Instructor Resource Center

GETTING REGISTERED

To register for the Instructor Resource Center, go to **www.pearsonhighered.com** and click **"Educators."**

1. Click **"Download teaching resources for your text"** in the blue welcome box.

2. Request access to download digital supplements by clicking the **"Request Access"** link. s

Follow the provided instructions. Once you have been verified as a valid Pearson instructor, an instructor code will be emailed to you. Please use this code to set up your Pearson login name and password. After you have set up your username and password, proceed to the directions below.

DOWNLOADING RESOURCES

1. Go to http://www.pearsonhighered.com/educator and use the "Search our catalog" option to find your text. You may search by Author, Title, or ISBN.

2. **Select your text** from the provided results.

Writing and Reading Across the Curriculum, 11/e
Behrens & Rosen
© 2011   Longman
ISBN-10: 0205727654

Part of series: Behrens/Rosen

3. After being directed to the catalog page for your text, click the **Instructor Resources** link located under the **Resources** tab.

   Clicking the Instructor Resources link will provide a list of all of the book-specific print and digital resources for your text below the main title. Items available for download will have a icon.

4. **Click on the View Downloadable Files** link next to the resource you want to download.

   A pop-up box will appear showing which files you have selected to download. Once you select the files, you will be prompted to login with an Instructor Resource Center login.

5. Enter you login name and password, and click the **"Submit"** button.

6. Read the terms and conditions and then click the **"I accept"** button to begin the download process.

   I accept (proceed with download)

   Cancel (closes this window)

7. **"Save"** the supplement file to a folder you can easily find again.

Once you are signed into the IRC, you may continue to download additional resources from our online catalog.

Please "Sign Out" when you are finished.

Meeting WPA Outcomes

The Council of Writing Program Administrators (WPA) statement on first-year composition programs outlines recommended goals for composition programs. While it is recognized that writing is a complex process that requires time and continued practice, the WPA does list outcomes for the first composition classes. (The full statement can be found at www.ilstu.edu/~ddhesse/wpa/positions/outcomes.htm. A version can also be found in *WPA: Writing Program Administration* 23.1/2 (1999): 59–66.)

Writing and Reading Across the Curriculum's approach provides students with ample practice in those areas that the WPA has identified as important outcomes: rhetorical knowledge; critical thinking, reading and writing; writing as a process; and knowledge of conventions. The writing assignment sequence of summary, critique, synthesis and analysis re-enforces the understanding of writing as a series of tasks. Each assignment allows students the opportunity to find, evaluate, analyze and synthesize primary and secondary sources. Students learn to "integrate their own ideas with those of others" and are encouraged to see the relationship "among language, knowledge, and power."

A Note on the Questions

Students should be advised to read the headnotes to master information about the author and the work that should be incorporated in some form into their syntheses and critiques.

There are two sets of questions in each chapter. One set (Review Questions, Discussion and Writing Suggestions) follows each reading selection. Another set (Synthesis Activities, Research Activities) follows the last set of Discussion and Writing Suggestions in each chapter.

The Review Questions call for factual responses based on the reading selection. Someone who has carefully read the selection should be able to correctly answer these questions in a few sentences. Review Questions are designed simply to facilitate recall and not to delve into the broader implications of the reading; they may be viewed as a helpful and necessary step in preparing a summary.

Discussion and Writing Suggestions are designed to stimulate further thought about the issues discussed in the reading selections; there are no "correct" answers, and answers are not necessarily confined within the boundaries of the reading selection itself. The Discussion and Writing Suggestions, therefore, should be helpful in preparing students to write syntheses or critiques. Or they may serve as alternative writing assignments to the Synthesis Activities. Used either exclusively or in combination with the Synthesis Activities, they allow the student to develop imaginative, personal, or simply less structured papers.

The Synthesis Activities at the end of each unit are designed to give the student practice in the skills that are the focus of Part I. Part I addresses how to develop a thesis and to incorporate multiple sources in a discussion. Chapter 4 introduces the concept of the explanatory synthesis and Chapter 5 continues with the argument synthesis. Chapter 6 introduces analysis and Chapter 7 shows how the skills practiced in Part I come together in the research paper. The Synthesis Activities in Part II provide the questions that encourage students to make connections among, and writing about, multiple sources on a single topic. Some of these Synthesis Activities involve analysis and some can be expanded into research activities. The Research Activities, also found at the end of each unit, suggest more connections and independent research related to the chapter topic and selections.

SAMPLE SYLLABI FOR
WRITING AND READING ACROSS THE CURRICULUM. ELEVENTH EDITION

SAMPLE SYLLABI

Here are sample syllabi, employing *Writing and Reading Across the Curriculum*, for a ten-week quarter and a fifteen-week semester. Naturally, the particular choice of chapter topics and the number of reading and writing assignments may be adjusted to suit the interests and needs of the particular class. In any case, we recommend no more than six or seven formal writing assignments during the course of a fifteen-week term. (Even if your students can handle more, you probably can't!) Other assignments may be informal, ungraded writing (or "quick-writes") done in notebooks. These may include journal entries and other prewriting activities, responses to the readings, or responses to the Review Questions and Discussion and Writing Suggestions following the readings. You may wish to schedule regular peer review sessions or other group work during which students respond to and evaluate one another's work in progress.

SYLLABUS 1

This syllabus assumes a ten-week course that meets three times per week. Students read the chapters in Part 1 and complete reading and writing assignments for three chapters in Part II.

WEEK 1
Reading Assignments
  A Note to the Student
  Chapter 1: *Summary, Paraphrase, and Quotation*
Writing Assignment
  Summary of either Coontz, "The Radical Idea of Marrying for Love," pp. 380–392 *or* Carskadon, "When Worlds Collide: Adolescent Need for Sleep Versus Societal Demands," pp. 493–501.

WEEK 2
Reading Assignment

Chapter 2: *Critical Reading and Critique*
Writing Assignment
Critique of either Ross and Nisbett, "The Power of Situations," pp. 688–692 *or* Sullivan or Bennett, "Debate on Gay Marriage," pp. 406–414.

WEEK 3
Reading Assignment
Chapter 3: *Introductions, Theses, and Conclusions*
Writing Assignment
Revision of either previously written summary or critique *or* additional summary or critique of a short article from a chapter in Part II.

WEEK 4
Reading Assignment
Chapter 4: *Explanatory Synthesis*
Chapter 8: *Green Power*
White, "Why the Gasoline Engine Isn't Going Away Soon"
Kolbert, "The Island in the Wind"
Burnett, "Wind Power Puffery"
Writing Assignment
Explanatory Synthesis *or* Chapter 8 Synthesis Activity

WEEK 5
Reading Assignment
Chapter 5: *Argument Synthesis*
Chapter 8: *Green Power* (continued)
Lemonick, "Global Warming: Beyond the Tipping Point"
Friedman, "205 Easy Ways to Save the Earth"
Gore, "The Climate for Change"
Bryce, "The Dangerous Delusions of Energy Independence"
Report of an Independent Task Force, "National Security Consequences of U.S. Oil Dependence"
Lubber, "Balance Sheets and the Climate Crisis: How American Business Can Help"
Maloney, "Environmentalists Against Solar Power"
Writing Assignment
Argument Synthesis #2, pp. 368–369 *or* complete work on Explanatory Synthesis *or* another Argument Synthesis activity from Chapter 8.

INSTRUCTOR'S MANUAL

to accompany

Behrens/Rosen

WRITING AND READING
ACROSS THE CURRICULUM

Eleventh Edition

RoseAnn Morgan
Middlesex County College

Longman

Upper Saddle River   Boston   Columbus   Indianapolis   New York   San Francisco

Toronto   Amsterdam   Cape Town   Dubai   London   Madrid   Milan   Munich   Paris   Montreal

Tokyo   Delhi   Mexico City   Sao Paulo   Sydney   Hong Kong   Seoul   Singapore   Taipei

Instructor's Manual to accompany Behrens/Rosen, *Writing and Reading Across the Curriculum,* Eleventh Edition

1 2 3 4 5 6 7 8 9 10 – BRR – 12 11 10 09

Longman is an
imprint of

www.pearsonhighered.com

ISBN 10: 0-205-73467-7
ISBN 13: 978-0-205-73467-2

CONTENTS

WEEK 6

Reading Assignment
  Chapter 6: *Analysis*
  Chapter 11: *New and Improved: Six Decades of Advertising*
  Fowles, "Advertising's Fifteen Basic Appeals"
  Bovée, Thill, Dovel, and Wood, "Making the Pitch in Print Advertising"
Writing Assignment
  Writing Suggestion following one or two of the readings in Chapter 11, or
  Synthesis Activity from Chapter 11.

WEEK 7

Reading Assignment
  Chapter 11: *New and Improved: Six Decades of Advertising* (continued)
  Bovée and Arens, "The Indictments against Advertising"
  A Portfolio of Print Advertisements
  A Portfolio of TV Commercials
Writing Assignment
  Begin selecting research topic; select from Research Activities from an
  assigned chapter in Part II in which you are interested, *or*
  Writing Suggestion following one or two of the readings in Chapter 11, *or*
  Synthesis Activity from Chapter 11.

WEEK 8

Reading Assignment
  Chapter 10: *To Sleep*
  Martin, "A Third of Life"
  Epstein, "Improving Sleep"
  National Sleep Foundation, "America's Sleep-Deprived Teens Nodding Off at
      School, Behind the Wheel"
  Carskadon, "When Worlds Collide"
  Dement and Vaughan, "Sleep Debt and the Mortgaged Mind"
Writing Assignment
  Continue developing research topic, *or*
  Writing Suggestion following one or two of the readings in Chapter 10, *or*
  Synthesis Activity from Chapter 10.

WEEK 9

  Reading Assignment
  Chapter 10: *To Sleep* (continued)

Buysse, "The Pittsburgh Sleep Quality Index"
Pilcher and Walters, "How Sleep Debt Hurts College Students"
Danner and Phillips, "Adolescent Sleep, School Start Times, and Teen Motor
    Vehicle Crashes"
Writing Assignment
    Draft research paper, *or*
    Writing Suggestion following one or two of the readings in Chapter 10, *or*
    Synthesis Activity from Chapter 10.

WEEK 10
Writing Assignment
    Conferences on research paper
    Oral reports/peer reviews for research paper
    Finish research paper

SYLLABUS 2

This syllabus, designed for a fifteen-week class, provides for more reading and writing assignments than Syllabus 1. The particular choice of chapter topics and the number of reading and writing assignments may be adjusted to suit the interests and needs of a particular class.

WEEK 1
Reading Assignment
    A Note to the Student
    Chapter 1: *Summary, Paraphrase, and Quotation*
Writing Assignment
    Summary of either Coontz, "The Radical Idea of Marrying for Love," pp. 380–
    392 *or* Carskadon, "When Worlds Collide: Adolescent Need for Sleep Versus
    Societal Demands," pp. 493-501.

WEEK 2
Reading Assignment
    Chapter 2: *Critical Reading and Critique*
Writing Assignment
    Critique of either Ross and Nisbett, "The Power of Situations," pp. 688–692 *or*
    Sullivan or Bennett, "Debate on Gay Marriage," pp. 406–414.

WEEK 3
Reading Assignment
 Chapter 3: *Introductions, Theses, and Conclusions*
Writing Assignment
 Revision of either previously written summary or critique *or* additional
 summary or critique of short article from chapter in Part II.

WEEK 4
Reading Assignment
 Chapter 4: *Explanatory Synthesis*
 Chapter 8: *Green Power*
 Zuckerman, "Stop the Energy Insanity"
 Sherman, "GM at 100: Is Its Future Electric?"
 White, "Why the Gasoline Engine Isn't Going Away Soon"
 Totty, "The Case For and Against Nuclear Power"
 Kolbert, "The Island in the Wind"
 Burnett, "Wind Power Puffery"
Writing Assignment
 Begin work on Explanatory Synthesis #1, p. 368, *or* Argument Synthesis #2
 p. 368 *or*
 any other Synthesis Activity.

WEEK 5
Reading Assignment
 Chapter 5: *Argument Synthesis*
 Chapter 8: *Green Power* (continued)
 Lemonick, "Global Warming: Beyond the Tipping Point"
 Friedman, "205 Easy Ways to Save the Earth"
 Bryce, "The Dangerous Delusions of Energy Independence"
 Report of an Independent Task Force, "National Security Consequences of
  U.S. Oil Dependence"
 Lubber, "Balance Sheets and the Climate Crisis: How American Business Can
  Help"
 Dickerson, "State Solar Power Plans Are as Big as All Outdoors"
 Maloney, "Environmentalists against Solar Power"
Writing Assignment
 Complete work on Explanatory Synthesis or Argument Synthesis Activity from
 Week 4.

WEEK 6
Reading Assignment
  Chapter 6: *Analysis*
  Chapter 11: *New and Improved: Six Decades of Advertising*
  Fowles, "Advertising's Fifteen Basic Appeals"
  Bovée, Thill, Dovel, and Wood, "Making the Pitch in Print Advertising"
  A Portfolio of Print Advertisements
  A Portfolio of TV Commercials
Writing Assignment
  Writing Suggestion following one or two of the readings in Chapter 11, or
  Synthesis Activity from Chapter 11.

WEEK 7
Reading Assignment
  Chapter 13: *Obedience to Authority*
  Fromm, "Disobedience as a Psychological and Moral Problem"
  Ross and Nisbett, "The Power of Situations"
  Milgram, "The Perils of Obedience"
Writing Assignment
  Writing Suggestion following one or two of the readings in Chapter 13.

WEEK 8
Reading Assignment
  Chapter 13: *Obedience to Authority* (continued)
  Parker, "Obedience"
  Lessing, "Group Minds'
  Asch, "Opinions and Social Pressure"
Writing Assignment
  Writing Suggestion following one or two of the readings in Chapter 13, *or*
  begin Synthesis Activity # 4, 6, 8 or 11 from Chapter 13.

WEEK 9
Reading Assignment
  Chapter 13: *Obedience to Authority* (continued)
  Zimbardo, "The Stanford Prison Experiment"
  McEwan, From *Atonement*

Writing Assignment
  Begin selecting research topic; select from Research Activities from an
  assigned chapter in Part II in which you are interested, *or*
  finish Synthesis Activity from Week 8.

WEEK 10
Reading Assignment
  Chapter 10: *To Sleep*
  Martin, "A Third of Life"
  National Sleep Foundation, "America's Sleep-Deprived Teens Nodding Off at
    School, Behind the Wheel"
  Carskadon, "When Worlds Collide: Adolescent Need for Sleep Versus Societal
    Demands"
Writing Assignment
  Begin research for research paper, *or*
  Writing Suggestion following one of the readings.

WEEK 11
Reading Assignment
  Chapter 10: *To Sleep* (continued)
  Dement and Vaughan, "Sleep Debt and the Mortgaged Mind"
  Pilcher and Walters, "How Sleep Debt Hurts College Students"
  Danner and Phillips, "Adolescent Sleep, School Start Times, and Teen Motor
    Vehicle Crashes"
Writing Assignments
  Continue research for research paper and continue drafting research paper, *or*
  Writing Suggestion following one of the major cases.

WEEK 12
Reading Assignment
  Chapter 7: *The Changing Landscape of Work in the Twenty-First Century*
  Huws, "Fixed and Footloose: Work and Identity in the Twenty-First Century"
  Judy and D'Amico, "Work and Workers in the Twenty-First Century"
  Friedman, "The Untouchables"
Writing Assignments
  Continue drafting research paper *or*
  Writing Suggestion following one of the readings.

WEEKS 13

Reading Assignment
  Chapter 7: *The Changing Landscape of Work in the Twenty-First Century*
  (continued)
  Blinder, "Will Your Job Be Exported?"
  The Economist, "Into the Unknown"
  Casner-Lotto and Barrington, "Are They Really Ready to Work?"
  Miller, "The Future of Engineering"
Writing Assignments
  Finish research paper *or*
  Writing Suggestion following one of the readings.

WEEKS 14 AND 15
  Conferences on research paper
  Oral reports re: research paper

A Note on MYCOMPLAB
and VIDEO LINKS

MYCOMPLAB

The Web site *MyCompLab* integrates the market-leading instruction, multimedia tutorials, and exercises for writing, grammar, and research that users have come to identify with the program, along with a new online composing space and new assessment tools. The result is a revolutionary application that offers a seamless and flexible teaching and learning environment built specifically for writers. Created by faculty and students across the country, the new MyCompLab provides help for writers in the context of their writing, with instructor and peer commenting functionality, proven tutorials and exercises for writing, grammar and research, an e-portfolio, an assignment-builder, a bibliography tool, tutoring services, and a gradebook and course management organization created specifically for writing classes. Visit www.mycomplab.com for information.

An e-book version of *Writing and Reading Across the Curriculum,* Part One, "How to Write Summaries, Critiques, Syntheses, and Analyses" is also available in MyCompLab. This online version of Part One integrates the many resources of MyCompLab, such as extra help with composing, researching, and documenting sources, thereby creating an enriched, interactive learning experience for writing students. This version additionally provides access to the videolinks correlated to each of thematic chapter as described in the *Instructor's Manual*.

MyCompLab provides topics in writing, grammar, and research. These resources are available to all users of MyCompLab, whether students are working on their own or in an instructor's course. MyCompLab organizes instruction, multimedia, and exercise content by topic. However, you also have access to a Media Index that organizes the content by type (for example, all videos in one list).

Each topic includes instructional, multimedia, and/or exercise resources.

- **Instructional resources** define concepts and provide examples of the concept. For some instructional resources, a QuickCheck appears at the end of an instruction. A QuickCheck is one or two questions or examples, and you select the correct answer or example. MyCompLab then displays a pop-up identifying whether your answer is correct or incorrect and why.

  For Pearson eText courses, the instructional resource list also has a link to the relevant section in the eText.

- **Multimedia resources**, when available, are typically audio clips or videos that reinforce a concept. The multimedia resources include animated and narrated tutorials that range from grammar topics, strategies for developing a draft, guidelines on peer reviews, and tutorials on avoiding plagiarism to deciding on the topic for a paper.

- **Exercises** provide you with the opportunity to practice and apply what you have learned. MyCompLab provides immediate feedback to your answers, letting you know whether your answer is correct or incorrect, which answer is correct, and why that answer is correct. MyCompLab also provides refresher resources to further reinforce the concept. The results of these exercises are logged in your Gradebook's Practice Results.

  Most topics have multiple sets of exercises to provide extensive practice. However, once you complete all the exercises for a topic, MyCompLab displays a **Take Again** link so you have the option of reworking a topic's exercises. The score you get when you retake the exercises replaces the original score.

TIP: A topic's exercises can be recommended by MyCompLab based on the results of a diagnostic assignment or by you when commenting on a student's writing submissions.

MyCompLab organizes instruction, multimedia, and exercise content by topic. However, you also have access to a Media Index that organizes the content by type (for example, all videos in one list).

VIDEO LINKS

In this Instructor's Manual, Chapters 7 through 13, we have provided video links that we hope will enhance the student's understanding and enjoyment of the material in that chapter. Most, if not all, of these videos are available on YouTube (YouTube.com). Using the indicated search terms on YouTube (or Google or Bing, if the videos are located elsewhere on the Web) will allow both you and the student to access these and related videos.

Note: Because Internet content frequently changes without warning, not all of the listed videos may be available when you attempt to access them. It is possible that errant searches may lead to other videos with objectionable content. Such videos, as well as user-submitted comments under videos do not reflect the views of the authors or of Pearson Publishing.

To cite these videos in a paper, students should use the format for online videos. Thus:

"Climate Change." *YouTube.* American Assn. of Science. n.d. Web. 26 Jan. 2008.

Chapter 1

Summary, Paraphrase, and Quotation

This chapter introduces students to the use of summary, paraphrase, and quotation—vital skills for many different kinds of writing both in college and in business. Writing a summary is the first assignment. Summarizing an entire article, either in the short or longer form, challenges students' reading and writing skills, and as such can work very effectively as a diagnostic of the their reading and writing skills. Summarizing allows students to gain mastery of content material as well as learn to be objective in reporting what they have read. Also, writing summaries allows students to practice in-text citation. Students may need to do two or more summaries before they feel comfortable with the process and before you are satisfied with their results. You may choose to grade these early summaries or just give them a check, check plus or check minus. I have found that it is a valuable learning experience—one which translates well to various kinds of assignments which come later in the semester—to have students practice summarizing a variety of things: expository material, persuasive writing (for which I often look to the editorial page of a major newspaper), and different kinds of graphs and tables of statistics. The textbook gives guidelines for summarizing all of these types of material.

After reading the examples presented in the textbook and studying the Guidelines for Writing Summaries, students should be encouraged to read the material to be summarized at least twice to identify the author's central idea before breaking the article into sections and writing a one-sentence summary of each section. The textbook examples can be referred to in order to demonstrate how to break down an argument into sections, and to show what a thesis statement looks like and how it works with topic sentences. If you wish to have students write longer summaries with multiple paragraphs, you can direct students to the sample papers on the textbook's Web site. Point out to students the necessity of transitions that clarify for the reader that this is a summary of someone else's ideas.

In summarizing, students must identify the author's main idea and then restate it in their own words. In some cases, students may attempt to summarize by only describing the content of the article rather than by capturing the author's ideas.

1

Stress the difference between what the author *does* in the article (e.g., the author might narrate or explain or describe something) and what the author *says* or claims. Additionally, have students examine their topic sentences to see if there is a dependence on "and then" types of transitional phrases. Such phrasing may indicate that the summary is merely describing what subjects the author addresses and not capturing the author's meaning. In the textbook, following each reading selection is a list of Review Questions. If you assign those readings to be summarized, the Review Questions can be used by your students to check their reading comprehension.

Working on the restatements (i.e., the one-sentence summaries of each section) necessary to produce a summary will move students away from too much dependence on direct quotations; such restatements also constitute a skill that will transfer to paraphrasing. The paraphrase differs from the summary in length and in more closely adhering to the author's organization and use of examples. Hence, the summary is always shorter than the original while the paraphrase may be the same length as the original. Students may be concerned about when to cite material at this point; explain that MLA requires parenthetic citations for both summaries and paraphrasing, but if one summarizes an entire work, the author's name and the title of the work should be given at the beginning of the summary. It is likely then that only a single parenthetic citation will be needed at the end of the summary or paraphrase to give a page number or numbers. If you allow direct quotations to be used in the summary, those quotations should be limited in number and length. Make sure that students understand the use of ellipses and brackets and that quotations are used sparingly rather than as substitutes for summary. Quoted material should also be smoothly and grammatically incorporated into students' writing. Signal phrases (attributive tags) are used to avoid freestanding quotations.

The following rubric, presented on the next page, is modified from that used at Central Washington University. It can be adapted to provide assessment criteria for the summary assignment.

ASSESSMENT GUIDE FOR SUMMARIES

Very Competent	Competent	Incompetent
*Summary is titled.	*Summary is titled.	*No title.
*Author, title, thesis clearly stated at the beginning of the summary.	*States the author and title, the thesis is accurately addressed (restated); perhaps an implied part of the thesis is missing; the author's thesis is restated in the writer's own words.	*Author and title never stated; no indication this is a summary.
*Author's purpose is clearly conveyed and restated in writer's own words.		*Reacts to content.
		*Misreads the author's thesis.
*Author's purpose is accurately presented.	*Restates all key ideas in the passage; some ideas may not be fully developed.	*Ideas are unclear; does not refer to key ideas; key ideas misquoted or misrepresented.
*Critical reading is evident.	*Usually restates the key ideas logically and coherently in the writer's own words; there may be gaps in coherence and/or logic, but the thesis is clear.	
*The writer sustains his/her discussion of the passage's objective.		*Lack of coherence (no order of ideas); relationship of ideas is unclear; does not express the complexity of the ideas; there are no transitions.
*Language is vibrant and vivid; the tone remains objective.	*Examples are given to support the key ideas made by the author in support of his/her thesis; these examples may not be complete.	
*Sentence structure is varied.		*No organization; main points are presented randomly or order describes the sequence of topics. No attempt is made to show relationship between thesis and support.
*Grammar reveals the writer's command of the written conventions of English.	*Gives the reader a clear sense of the contents of the passage.	
	*Contains topic sentences that present controlling ideas.	
	*Free from serious mechanical errors. Errors do not distract the reader or impede reading.	*Vague language, vague references; does not convey ideas clearly.
		*Uses author's language.
		*Mechanical errors.

3

STUDENT WEB RESOURCES

UNIVERSITY OF VICTORIA ENGLISH DEPARTMENT. THE UVIC WRITER'S GUIDE:
This site provides instructions on writing summaries and includes samples.
http://Web.uvic.ca/wguide/Pages/summariesTOC.html

PURDUE UNIVERSITY. PURDUE ONLINE WRITING LAB: QUOTING,
PARAPHRASING, AND SUMMARIZING
This site discusses quotations, paraphrases, and summaries, including definitions
of the terms. A practice exercise is included as well.
http://owl.english.purdue.edu/handouts/research/r_quotprsum.html

C. SANDRA JAMIESON. DREW UNIVERSITY. RESOURCES FOR WRITERS:
SUMMARY WRITING
This is a varied and valuable site which explains the importance of summarizing
as a necessary component of most other kinds of writing as well as its importance
in note taking.
http://www.users.drew.edu/~sjamieso/summary.html

JACKSON STATE COMMUNITY COLLEGE
This site provides a good, concise outline of how to write summaries. The site
also provides links to writing thesis statements and topic sentences as well as
how to avoid plagiarism.
http://www.jscc.edu/academics/programs/writingcenter/resources2/
summarizing.html

THE HUNTER COLLEGE READING/WRITING CENTER
This site describes the qualities of a good summary and provides clear and
detailed instructions for producing good summaries.
http://courses.washington.edu/ordinary/summary.pdf

Chapter 2

Critical Reading and Critique

Having worked with the summary, students should now be able to identify the purpose, structure and thesis in an article and be able to formulate their own thesis. In the textbook, exercises in Chapter 2 provide practice in critical reading and writing to help direct students in the process. In preparation for the later synthesis assignments, students will need to recognize the difference between informative (expository) and persuasive writing as well as informative and persuasive thesis statements. Exercise 2.1 in the textbook will help them understand those differences. Incorporating summary, the critique assignment requires that students both understand what they have read and evaluate it. They should have summarized some articles pertaining to the topic of the critique before attempting the critique itself in order to be able to succeed at evaluating what they have read. As some students may interpret the word "critique" to mean a harsh attack on something, it may be necessary to stress that a critique is an evaluation or an assessment, and that it can be positive.

In Chapter 2, Alan S. Blinder's "Will Your Job Be Exported?" provides the basis for a model critique that examines the following assertion: In a global economy, the stability of jobs in the U.S. workforce will come to depend less on college-level training (as was the case in the past) and more on the nature of the job itself. Work that requires a direct human presence (e.g., surgeon, barber, plumber, undertaker) will tend to be stable, while work that can be automated or shipped offshore (e.g., accounting, some types of law, data entry) will tend to be less stable.

Many articles in the Anthology of Readings will work as subjects of critiques. In creating a critique, students should first ask what assumptions the author holds. Then students should determine whether those assumptions are valid by asking whether the information presented is accurate and significant, whether the information has been presented logically and fairly, and whether the author has defined key terms clearly and unambiguously. Only after students have answered these questions and made notes should they proceed with writing the critique. In their critiques, students may agree or disagree with what they have read, or they may do some of both—agreeing with part of the article and disagreeing with

5

another part. In any case, students must adhere to the process of critiquing; simply endorsing or opposing what the writer has said is not sufficient.

Since students have already worked on summarizing, they might get bogged down when summarizing a source for the critique. Emphasize that the purpose here is to summarize only the author's key points, particularly those that will be discussed in the critique, and that the analysis and evaluation should comprise the bulk of the critique.

While students may believe they have arrived at their evaluation when they begin writing the critique, the writing process often gives them the opportunity to rethink their evaluation and allow them to change their minds as they write. Because of this, students need to be reminded to continually examine their thesis statement in the drafting process and reword it as necessary.

This assignment presents a good opportunity for students to start documenting with in-text references.

The following checklist can be used in peer review workshops for the critique paper.

PEER FEEDBACK CHECKLIST: CRITIQUE

Does the critique

_____   introduce and clearly identify author, title of article, and subject matter?

_____   identify the author's thesis and purpose?

_____   state, within the first two paragraphs, the student's position (evaluation) along with the points the student intends to address?

_____   restate the author's key ideas logically and concisely in the student's own words?

_____   restate the author's ideas accurately?

_____   examine the author's assumptions?

____ analyze the author's language and logic in detail, supported by references to the text?

____ establish a clear relationship between the author's thesis and the student's evaluation points?

____ evaluate the strengths of the article before proceeding to evaluate its weaknesses?

____ combine analysis of the article with response to the author's argument?

____ maintain an objective tone?

____ quote accurately and indicate changes to quotes with ellipses or brackets?

STUDENT RESOURCES

ACADEMIC WRITING: CRITICAL REVIEWS
The Writing Center at the University of Wisconsin-Madison provides many helpful links for various writing assignments, one of which is a critique.
http://www.wisc.edu/writing/Handbook/CriNonfiction.html

THE WRITING TUTORIAL SERVICES AT INDIANA UNIVERSITY, BLOOMINGTON
This site provides a good discussion of critiquing a book under "Writing Book Reviews." Most of the points discussed here can be applied to critiquing an article or essay.
http://www.indiana.edu/~wts/wts/bookreview.html

Understanding fallacies and being able to identify them is an important part of a critique. The following two sites complement the discussion of fallacies in *WRAC*.

"STEPHEN'S GUIDE TO THE LOGICAL FALLACIES" BY STEPHEN DOWNES
This is a comprehensive site that explains and provides numerous examples of logical fallacies.
http://onegoodmove.org/fallacy/

7

THE FALLACY FILES

This is a comprehensive site that provides explanations of fallacies with examples from books, newspapers, magazines, newsletters, and fundraising letters.

http://www.fallacyfiles.org

Chapter 3

Introductions, Theses, and Conclusions

This chapter addresses some of the most difficult elements of a paper: the introduction, the thesis, and the conclusion. The introduction establishes the context, the general idea of the paper, as well as the mood, tone, and general approach. *WRAC* suggests a number of effective strategies for creating an introduction: providing a provocative quotation, providing historical background, reviewing a controversy, arranging ideas from the general to the specific or from the specific to the general, asking a question, or simply starting with the thesis statement itself.

As the controlling idea of a paper, the thesis statement serves to help students focus on their supporting ideas more effectively. Of the three types of thesis statements (explanatory, mildly argumentative, and strongly argumentative), it is probably best to begin with the explanatory thesis and practice the others in later assignments. When students work on drafts of thesis statements in class or individually, they quickly realize that they can effectively control their ideas before committing themselves to full drafts. Working thesis statements can be discussed in peer-review groups or placed on the board during a thesis workshop for class discussion and revision. Have the students bring to class a sentence with a claim and a support clause (a "because clause"). After examining these sample thesis statements, students can suggest ways that the statements may be narrowed or broadened and then be made mildly or strongly argumentative. Once students develop well-crafted theses, choose one to show how it contains all the information needed to create an outline for an essay. (Creating an outline from a thesis statement is covered in Chapter 5; you may want to wait until then to engage in this.)

The thesis workshop also gives you an opportunity to check on how well prepared students are for writing their papers. Students who are well prepared will be able to state and explain their positions; less well-prepared students will offer vague statements or fail to make a claim. Check working thesis statements for poor reasoning and alert students if they are only redefining the language of the claim in their support clause.

9

Next, this chapter offers suggestions for concluding a paper. Urge students to see the introduction and conclusion as working together: the introduction acts like a bridge, bringing the reader into the world of the paper, while the conclusion reverses the process and takes the reader back out into the world. Because of this, unless the paper is quite long the conclusion should not simply repeat the thesis statement and topics sentences. Rather, it should take a larger or more outward-looking approach by pointing out the significance of what has been discussed; calling for further research; suggesting a solution to the problem or making a recommendation; delivering a memorable anecdote or quotation; asking a pertinent question; or by speculating on what might happen regarding what has been discussed. Some students will end their papers with a "but everyone has their own opinions" sort of conclusion. Stress that they should make their case and go out strong, not undermine their own argument.

STUDENT WEB RESOURCES

The Thesis Statement
PURDUE UNIVERSITY'S ONLINE WRITING LAB (OWL)
Purdue University's site provides "Tips and Examples for Writing Your Thesis Statement." This site offers some of the fullest, most reliable writing assistance available online.
> http://owl.english.purdue.edu/owl/resource/545/01

Online Handouts: Introductions and Conclusions
ARIZONA STATE UNIVERSITY
This site provides dozens of handouts that can be downloaded, including some on introductions and conclusions along with various strategies to create a successful paper.
> http://studentsuccess.asu.edu/writing/resources

Introductions and Conclusions
CLEVELAND STATE UNIVERSITY WRITING CENTER
This writing center site provides some good tips on writing introductions and conclusions as well as giving examples of each via the links near the bottom of the page.
> http://www.csuohio.edu/writingcenter/introcnc.html

Strategies for Writing a Conclusion
ST. CLOUD STATE UNIVERSITY, LEO (LITERACY EDUCATION ONLINE)
This site from St. Cloud State University gives a good, clear discussion of various conclusion strategies and examples of each.
> http://leo.stcloudstate.edu/acadwrite/conclude.html

10

Chapter 4

Explanatory Synthesis

Writing syntheses is covered in two chapters: Chapter 4 introduces the genre and focuses on the explanatory synthesis; Chapter 5 is devoted to the argument synthesis.

Stress to students that in writing syntheses they are extending what they have already learned and practiced in writing summaries and critiques. As with critiques, the synthesis requires that students summarize sources and evaluate them. But the new element here is that a synthesis is based on more than one source, so students must identify and understand the relationship between or among the sources. A difficulty that students may have is in doing just that— identifying the relationship between or among sources.

Selecting sources is the first step, but if the authors' views are too similar, the synthesis may become just a list of comparable points. If the authors' views are too different, synthesizing those views might be almost impossible. The idea is to select authors whose ideas are similar enough for discussion but different enough to create some tension in the paper. Students should ask, "What will my readers realize or learn by my bringing these sources together that they would not realize or learn by reading them separately?"

The explanatory synthesis is informative. This, however, does not mean there is neither purpose nor thesis. Students need to understand why these sources are being brought together and then formulate a thesis that narrows the topic into a declarative statement. The thesis, like the student model in this chapter of the textbook, may indicate the basic differences between the two sources.

To show how a synthesis is developed, Behrens and Rosen briefly excerpt a number of sources. Students should be reminded, though, that they will need to work from entire articles when they do their own research. If they wish to make use of any of the excerpted selections, they need to use the provided citations to track down the original. Following the readings, a student—Janice Hunte— discusses her approach to organizing the sources and drafting an initial thesis. (Students should note that the cited page numbers refer to the original sources,

11

i.e., Hunte tracked down the full text of all of the original sources excerpted in *WRAC*.) After summarizing points from the readings, she is able to develop an outline for her synthesis with topic sentences. Note that Hunte's outline is organized according to ideas, not the sources. The textbook provides essential and helpful advice regarding organizing a synthesis: Organizing by a series of source summaries is incorrect; organizing by ideas and referring to the relevant parts of multiple sources is correct. Next, the first draft of the synthesis is presented with instructor's suggestions for revision. In Exercise 4.3, students are offered a chance to revise the draft themselves before examining how the revisions were handled in the model paper. As with all the model papers, the highlighted thesis statement and topic sentences emphasize how these elements create clear, strong structure. The model synthesis also provides examples of how to incorporate quotations and use in-text citations. Point out the format for an indirect quotation (a commonly asked question regarding documentation) and the examples of electronically accessed sources.

The following checklist can be used for students to check their own work or in a peer-review workshop on the explanatory synthesis.

PEER FEEDBACK CHECKLIST: SYNTHESIS

_____ Does the synthesis introduce and clearly identify the material and author under analysis?

_____ Is the student's purpose identified?

_____ Does the thesis statement name the points that the student intends to address?

_____ Does the organization show how the sources relate to one another?

_____ Are the key ideas of the sources presented logically, concisely, and accurately in the student's own words?

_____ Are the authors' assumptions examined?

_____ Is it clear which author is being referred to?

12

_____ Are the language and logic of the authors analyzed and supported by references to the text?

_____ Is there a clear relationship between the student's thesis and each major point in the synthesis?

_____ Does the student's response to the authors' ideas connect with the analysis?

_____ Are the student's tone and language objective?

_____ Are quotes accurate? Have any changes been signaled by brackets and ellipses?

_____ Are quotations and paraphrases correctly documented?

_____ Is sentence structure varied? Are transitional words and phrases used effectively?

_____ Is word choice effective and free of clichés and jargon?

_____ Is the synthesis free of serious mechanical and grammatical errors?

STUDENT WEB RESOURCES

Resources for Writers: Synthesis Writing
DREW UNIVERSITY
C. Sandra Jamieson discusses synthesis writing prefaced by short discussions of "Synthesis Writing Outside of College."
        http://www.users.drew.edu/~sjamieso/Synthesis.htm#key%20features

SNOW COLLEGE
This site provides a thirty-five page online handbook covering a wide range of writing topics, including the writing of syntheses.
        http://www.snow.edu/~jeffc/handbook.pdf

PEARSON EDUCATION
Examples of MLA in-text citations and Works Cited entries can be found at
        http://www.pearsoneducation.com/mla

Chapter 5

Argument Synthesis

The major difference between the explanatory synthesis and the argument synthesis is one of purpose: the explanatory synthesis seeks to inform while the argument synthesis seeks to persuade. Each type requires a clear thesis statement, and although all theses may be seen as argumentative to some extent, the thesis for the argument synthesis is persuasive in purpose while the thesis for the explanatory synthesis is, according to Behrens and Rosen, "fairly modest in purpose. It emphasizes the sources themselves, not the writer's use of sources to persuade others." In this chapter, students are introduced to the elements of persuasion. Guidance is provided for developing and organizing support. Additionally, an annotated model paper highlights and discusses the use of argumentative strategies.

The chapter begins with a formal definition of the thesis as a logical statement, showing how it contains a claim (the thesis statement) and convincing support for that claim. The claim and its support are linked by the writer's assumption about the claim; it is the writer's assumption—the writer's underlying belief—(often unstated) which gives the thesis statement its edge. Following a discussion of the logical elements of argument, students are presented with an overview of the three classical appeals: *logos*, *ethos*, and *pathos*. Each category is then explored with examples. A discussion and examples of deductive and inductive reasoning are given in the explanation of *logos*.

Next, a series of readings is presented on the subject of "Balancing Privacy and Safety in the Wake of Virginia Tech." These readings provide students with an opportunity to practice looking for and identifying logical fallacies and argumentative appeals before writing their argument synthesis. Once again, the thesis statement plays a crucial role since a well-formulated and well-worded thesis statement will present a rough outline of how to organize the argument synthesis. Also, students must consider the claim, support, and assumption (underlying belief) that form the backbone of the paper. They may also make a *concession* to an author's opposing ideas by accepting wholly or in part what the author has written. In making such a concession, students should consider what *counterarguments* can be raised against their position, admit that some of these

14

counterarguments may be valid, and then offer an alternative or a solution to the counterarguments. As in the previous chapter, this chapter contains a model documented paper based on the model thesis and outline. The model paper is followed by a paragraph-by-paragraph analysis of its argument and the various appeals the writer has used. By studying these, students can gain insight into the strategies used by the writer.

While more experienced writers will intuitively know how to develop and balance rational appeals (i.e., source evidence) and motivational appeals, less skilled writers will need help in sorting out how to order material in their papers. Chapter 5 provides examples of different types of argument patterns and then concludes with sample comparison-contrast outlines using source and criteria organization.

The Peer Feedback Checklist at the end of the previous chapter can be modified for a peer-review workshop that is focused an argument synthesis.

STUDENT WEB RESOURCES

Argumentation and Persuasion

PURDUE, OWL
The following resource discusses logic within writing, especially vocabulary and *logos*-based reasoning. It also covers logical fallacies.
   http://owl.english.purdue.edu/handouts/general/gl_argpers.html

THE UNIVERSITY OF NORTH CAROLINA AT CHAPEL HILL
The following site discusses *ethos*, *pathos*, and *logos* in detail and provides pointers on how to use them effectively.
   http://www.unc.edu/~hee/web11fall99/rhetoric.htm

For Web sites that discuss and give examples of logical fallacies, see the sites at the end of Chapter 2 in this Manual.

Chapter 6

Analysis

Many students will successfully master the summary and the critique, the first of which focuses on restating and the second of which focuses on restating and evaluating. Students may be mystified, however, when their instructors ask them to analyze: to *use* (not merely to summarize or critique) a reading selection as a tool for understanding phenomena in the world: their own experience, other readings, current events, objects in nature, and more. Chapter 6 explains how to do this.

The chapter begins by showing students how to identify in source material a principle or definition that they can use as an analytical tool. Students who understand that the purpose of an analysis is to reveal something will understand how two authors, using different analytical tools, can explore very different views of the same subject.

Students will find two demonstrations of analysis in the chapter. Marie Winn's "The Plug-In Drug" identifies elements of addiction and applies them to TV viewing. Winn concludes, according to her definition, that television viewing can be understood as an addiction. In the next example analysis, student Edward Peselman provides an example of an analysis written in response to a class assignment. He draws on sociologist Randall Collins's definition of the exercise of power to analyze the power relationships among a group of students in a freshman dorm.

After studying these two papers, students can practice finding principles and definitions for analysis in the reading selections of Part II. To identify principles and definitions, students need to look for 1) a concluding general statement that suggests a rule or law or 2) a definition that proposes a way of breaking down a term.

The thesis of Peselman's analysis is developed in two parts: the first part establishes the validity of the principle or definition to the subject under examination. Once the thesis is established, it is possible to draft an organizational plan by developing questions based on the applicable definition or

16

principle and applying those questions to the subject being investigated. Students should expect to write at least two drafts of their analysis.

Students sometimes blame their writing problems on a lack of interest in their topic. Peselman's paper shows that one's own experiences can provide valuable contributions to a paper and that writing can be a means of coming to terms with life experiences. His thoughtful analysis of a personal experience allows him to understand his own and others' extreme behaviors.

The boxed "Guidelines for Writing Analyses" break the analysis down into four parts, each of which is important to the success of the finished analysis. A common student error at this point, as with the critique, is to produce a summary rather than an analysis. Emphasize that students must reach a valid conclusion based on the principle or definition used to construct the analysis. They must commit themselves to and defend a claim. The chapter shows them how to do so.

Students should also check to make sure that they have delivered what they promised when introducing their definition or principle. Once the analytical principle or definition has been discussed, it should be applied systematically throughout the paper. Students in peer groups can ask each other if the analysis provides insight that goes beyond the obvious.

And while few sources are used in an analysis, those that are used must be correctly documented; quotations, paraphrase, and any summary should be carefully checked to ensure that sources are being used accurately.

STUDENT WEB RESOURCES.

HUNTER COLLEGE WRITING CENTER/WRITING ACROSS THE
CURRICULUM/HUMANITIES: WRITING ABOUT ART
This handout provides pertinent questions for students to consider when analyzing painting, sculpture, or architecture.
http://rwc.hunter.cuny.edu/reading-writing/on-line/writeart.html

THINKING CRITICALLY ABOUT WORLD WIDE WEB RESOURCES
At this UCLA Library site, Esther Grassian provides criteria to consider when analyzing Web sites and sources from Web sites.
http://www.library.ucla.edu/libraries/college/11605_12337.cfm

Chapter 7

The Changing Landscape of Work in the Twenty-first Century

The chapter opens with a series of definitions—of work, career, profession, and vocation—relevant to topics in the reading selections that follow. Next is Ursula Huws' article on "fixed," "footloose," and "fractured" jobs. Then Richard Sennett focuses on a single person to highlight the costs of the new job marketplace. This is followed by Tom Peters' article which outlines six survival skills needed in this new marketplace. Richard W. Judy and Carol D'Amico outline four major forces in the coming job market. Next, Thomas L. Friedman suggests three categories that will help secure employment and income in a globalized economy. Alan S. Blinder keys into some of the same points made by Friedman and makes suggestions of how to keep certain areas of employment secure. The article from *The Economist* asks "Where will the jobs of the future come from?" The next selection, the Bureau of Labor Statistics provides information on "Tomorrow's Jobs." Then Jill Casner-Lotto and Linda Barrington ask of both high-school and college graduates "Are They Really Ready to Work?" and give the answer: no. Richard K. Miller points out important changes in the field of engineering, including the need for engineers to excel in non-technical areas. The chapter ends with Tom McGrath and Matt Richtel discussing changes in law and medicine, respectively, regarding corporate profits vs. a comfortable work week.

In addition, the chapter includes multiple video supplements to the readings. These are listed at the end of this chapter. Note: the video "The Other Side of Outsourcing," with Thomas Friedman, would enhance the reading of "The Untouchables."

Definitions: Work, Career, Profession, Vocation (p. 213)

Definitions of the above terms by different authors create a basis for understanding much of what is discussed in various selections throughout the chapter.

18

REVIEW QUESTIONS

1. Both Thomas and Ciulla note that people understand work as an activity that *must* be done—that is a necessity. Ciulla distinguishes between external and internal necessity. *External* necessity provides a motivation to work from outside the worker—the demands of an employer, the need for money, etc. *Internal* necessity is the motivation of the artist or the monk in meditation, the need to work to satisfy a private desire.

2. The Bible regards work as a punishment for disobedience. In 528, Benedictine monks helped to transform that view by regarding work as a form of prayer. In the seventeenth century, Puritans further sacralized work by claiming that the accumulation of wealth was a sign of God's favor.

3. In the nineteenth century, the word *career* came to be understood as "a pre-established total pattern of organized professional activity, with upward movement through recognized preparatory stages and advancement based on merit" (Bledstein). That definition held for much of the twentieth century until the forces of globalization fundamentally changed the relationship between worker and employer and worker and work. Today a *career* does not imply a worker's commitment to a single type of work, a single skill set, or a single employer. Nor does a career denote a pre-determined track of professional activity. Instead, the twenty-first-century worker's career may involve different jobs that require differing skills and a near-constant learning of new techniques to remain current and employable. In the twenty-first century, a career is invented and discovered, in process, by the worker; in the nineteenth and (much of the) twentieth centuries, career paths were largely set in advance.

4. A profession (see Carter) is work that requires mastery of a body of specialized knowledge. A profession is a largely self-organized and self-policing community of practitioners who are responsible for training and admitting new practitioners. Professionals show concern for the greater good and enjoy high social esteem.

5. A vocation is what Ciulla would term work that is borne of an inner necessity, a passion for work that completes one's sense of self—work that a person "can't *not* do" (Guilford). A vocation may have a spiritual and religious dimension as well—as work one feels "called" to do based on principles of faith (Pope John Paul II).

19

Fixed and Footloose: Work and Identity in the Twenty-First Century (p. 214).

URSULA HUWS

Sociologist Ursula Huws describes the rapid changes that can occur in the workforce as jobs "are created (and disappear) with great rapidity." In this employment landscape, she identifies "fixed," "footloose," and "fractured" jobs.

REVIEW QUESTIONS

1. The fourth paragraph is a descriptive, fact-based overview of changes in the workplace—an overview that will be supported by evidence in the paper that follows. The fourth paragraph is value-neutral, and we cannot find Huws using a single word that implies a judgment about the many changes she sees. In her final paragraph, however, she makes firm judgments about these changes, and her anxiety and her condemnation are clear. First, she caricatures the old, hierarchical world of work as rigid and potentially unfair to women and minorities. The old world of work had its problems—but in saying that a caricature is "easy," Huws implies that the caricature is at least partially flawed and that there were benefits, too, to the old way of organizing work. Without the old rules to stabilize an individual's identity and promote values such as trust and mutual dependence, the new workplace threatens workers with personal and social havoc, the particulars of which Huws sets up (powerfully) in the second part of her final paragraph. We see in her multiple answers to her organizing "what do we have?" evidence that Huws is not neutral. She is alarmed; she sees a social order (even though flawed) crumbling; she implies a condemnation that she does not make explicit.

2. See especially the third, fourth, and final paragraphs of Huws's paper. Traditionally, one's job anchored both identity as a worker and one's place in the larger social order. The job traditionally provided "skills for life" and a "recognized position in the social division of labor." Changes in technology and globalization have caused an "upheaval" both for the individual's job security and his/her sense of social identity. When a person's job is outsourced or rendered obsolete by computers, he/she loses not only a livelihood but also an identity and a sense of purpose. Those fortunate enough to retain jobs also face problems because the fiercely globalized marketplace constantly threatens to eliminate jobs. To maintain livelihoods, workers may be asked to master new skills and discard old ones that were

sources of pride and a stable social identity. Moreover, one-time friends and colleagues, looking to safeguard their own welfare in the newly unstable workplace, may become potential competitors—possible threats to job security. These changes, says Huws, create upheaval in the lives of workers.

3. "Fixed" work is work that "has previously been geographically tied to a particular place." Examples of fixed work would be a food worker, surgeon, or barber—jobs that require "the need for physical proximity to a particular spot." Historically, fixed work was done by local people, rooted to the place they worked. Changes in technology (cheap travel, for instance) and globalization have brought people from across the globe to take on traditionally fixed work—and so we now have the phenomenon of "footloose" workers taking on "fixed" jobs.

4. "Footloose" work is work completed by workers far from the locales where a finished product of that work will be used or sold. Footloose work has had deep historical roots in the trading of goods between regions, since ancient times. Today, transnational companies distribute work across the globe in search of low labor and production costs (see paragraph 12). Historically, footloose work was related to manufacturing. More recently, both low- and high-skill white-collar work (such as data entry or computer programming) has been sent offshore as companies try to save money. "eOutsourcing" has become an important mechanism by which work, once local and fixed, has become footloose. The "paradigmatic case of footlooseness [has become work that slides] without friction between teams across the globe who are linked by telecommunications networks" (paragraph 15).

5. See paragraphs 16-18. "Fractured" work is work that exhibits qualities of fixed and footloose work that "are in constant, tense interaction with each other." In a fractured existence, work that has been distributed across time zones (that is, footloose work) creates demands on people doing fixed work. For example, work distributed to India requires workers in London or New York to be available twenty-four hours a day. This, in turn, creates a round-the-clock economy in which stores stay open through the night to service the needs of night-shift workers. In a personal sense, fixed interactions such as cleaning a house or playing with a child are interrupted by the virtual demands of phone calls and email. In a fractured job, the worker is always "on," and the boundaries between work and not-work blur: work is taken

21

home; work is completed while the worker eats lunch or sits in a taxi on the way to the airport.

No Long Term: New Work and the Corrosion of Character (p. 220)
RICHARD SENNETT

Sociologist Richard Sennett describes both the generational changes that have occurred in work and the demands on oneself and one's family in the new economy. Sennett tells us about Enrico, the janitor who worked hard so that his children could have a better future, and Rico, Enrico's son, who has achieved what his father wanted but at some cost to employment stability and family togetherness.

REVIEW QUESTIONS

1. "No long term" is shorthand for a fundamental change in the way businesses interact with workers. During the approximately thirty years following the Second World War, there thrived an implicit long-term contract between employer and employee: a worker learned a core set of skills, held more or less the same job for a lifetime, advanced through a career showing loyalty to the company, then retired. "Long-term" made for a stable, orderly working life. "No long term" upends this stability. Organizations expect workers to learn new skills sets demanded by new projects and adapt to working on short-term, networked teams that come together for projects and then disband to form new teams that follow new projects around the globe. In "No long term," reciprocal loyalty between employee and employer and also between employees themselves disappears. *Change* becomes the constant in "No long term," evidence of which is this: "a young American with at least two years of college can expect to change jobs at least eleven times in the course of working, and change his or her skill base at least three times during those forty years of labor."

2. Enrico, the father, and Rico, the son, have very different life narratives. The father held one job as a janitor for forty years. He pursued the American dream paycheck by paycheck investing his life and labor in a steady job that would provide benefits less for himself than for his children who, he hoped, would attend college so that they would never have to be janitors. Protected by unions and an economy that rewarded a steady, loyal work ethic, Enrico thrived—incrementally. Over time, he paid for a house in the suburbs but also maintained his connections with the "old neighborhood," where he was

22

lauded as a local son who succeeded in the broader world. Enrico strongly valued commitment, loyalty, and fidelity—both to work and to family. Rico, by contrast, seems adrift in the new economy, believing in his father's values but unable to demonstrate them to his children in a new economy that espouses "chameleon values": no commitment or loyalty; no trust; no pride in a skill set; no sacrifice. He has moved his family four times pursuing different jobs. Employers have made no commitment to him and he, in turn, finds it impossible to demonstrate through his own lack of commitment to work the values he wants to pass on to his children. On the face of things, Rico has succeeded economically; but the very "flexible behavior which has brought him success is weakening his own character in ways for which there exists no practical remedy" (paragraph 43).

3. See paragraphs 26-30. Organizations are flattening in the new economy. Old, top-down hierarchies in which senior managers made all decisions are being disbanded in favor of flatter, less bureaucratic network-like groups in which decision-making occurs at the group level. Work has become "contingent" and based on short-term "projects"—not (the old word) "jobs," which implied a steady, fixed labor force. Working teams come together for projects then disband and reform for others. Job-based stability inside the organization is lost as companies increasingly focus on moving nimbly from one short-term project to the next.

4. Rico feels himself set adrift in a corporate culture that no longer rewards or even acknowledges as useful the values he was raised by and sees as central in raising his children. He therefore wants to protect his family from "short-term" values. Moreover, Rico sees the "emphasis on teamwork and open discussion" (see paragraph 36) so highly valued in the workplace as being poisonous to family relations when parents evade their responsibilities as decision makers and regard children their moral and ethical equals. Rico exclaims: "Things have to hold together." But with respect to the values he holds more dearly, things are not holding together. He believes the "chameleon values" and behaviors demanded by the new economy threaten his family members, and he feels the need to protect them.

5. Rico's dilemma is that the very qualities he has developed to succeed in the new economy threaten to corrode his character.

I Feel So Damn Lucky! (p. 230)

TOM PETERS

In the new workplace, an office worker cannot assume job security. Management consultant Tom Peters says that these office workers must have six specific "survival skills."

REVIEW QUESTIONS

1. According to Peters, the workplace of the 1950s and '60s rewarded loyalty and rote performance. The new world of work abandons that stability and inefficiency in favor of an ability to adapt to rapidly changing conditions. Whereas work in the old world meant being stuck in the "[s]ame processes" with the same people, new work calls for collaborations among workers across the globe who—depending on skill sets needed—continually form and re-form project teams to meet changing demands.

2. Peters names six survival skills. *Mastery*: a particular field of excellence that distinguishes a worker from others; *Contacts*: a list of peers worldwide who can be trusted to form work for specific tasks; *Entrepreneurial instinct*: a nose for business that positions the alert, ambitious worker to learn about and seize opportunities; *Love of technology*: not just comfort with changing technologies but a commitment to staying current with emerging technologies; *Marketing*: a facility for self-promotion that alerts others to your skills; *Passion for renewal*: a commitment to continually learn and improve.

3. Peters uses a sports analogy to suggest that, as is the case with athletes, workers in the twenty-first century will be evaluated on their latest performance, not on a lengthy or honored history of performance. Workers are welcome so long as they produce; when they don't or can't, they will be released—just as athletes are. The system may be brutal, but it assures success.

Work and Workers in the Twenty-first Century (p. 233)

RICHARD W. JUDY AND CAROL D'AMICO

Writing for the Hudson Institute, Richard W. Judy and Carol D'Amico outline four major changes that will face twenty-first-century workers: the impact of technological change, globalization, the aging of America's baby boomers, and the inclusion of greater numbers of minorities in the labor force.

REVIEW QUESTIONS

1. According to the Hudson Institute (see paragraph 4), the first of two distinguishing qualities will be the disappearance of discrimination (age, gender, race) that discourages employment opportunities. Discrimination will disappear due to enlightened self-interest of employers looking for the best possible workers. The second distinguishing quality will be the disappearance of long-term commitments between employees and companies, unions, and the government. Employment is more likely to be free-lance in nature.

2. According to researchers at the Hudson Institute, four "forces" will influence the contours of future work: the pace of technological change; the globalization of the American economy; the aging of the American workforce; and the ethnic diversification (albeit slow) of the American labor force.

3. The future workforce will be highly mechanized and highly technical. Work requiring brute strength will be handled by machine or sent offshore. American workers who want good jobs will need to be "sophisticated" in order to compete for the good jobs that remain.

4. The economies of the world are linked today, and one cannot talk of the U.S. economy without discussing the world economy. Knowledge, data, and money cross borders without cost—with a consequence for workers: Highly-skilled workers who manufacture specialty goods for export will do well as demand for U.S. goods rises. Low-skilled workers will be hit hard by competition from low-paid workers overseas. The service industries will flourish as manufacturing jobs disappear. In a rising number of small-companies poised to take advantage of a volatile economy, highly skilled

25

workers will flourish while low-skilled workers and union membership will suffer.

5. The aging of baby boomers will affect workers who must pay to maintain shaky entitlement programs such as Medicare. Increased life spans will result in many older people remaining longer in the workforce in flexible work arrangements. As boomers age, their needs in retirement for leisure and care will create an opportunity for the service economy, which will replace many low-skilled manufacturing jobs lost to competition overseas.

6. The "skills premium" refers to the fate of workers who, through schooling and technological training, are adaptable in their work and will succeed in the global economy. Those with minimal skills will fill low-end service jobs.

The Untouchables (p. 238)

THOMAS L. FRIEDMAN

By "untouchable," Thomas L. Friedman means jobs that cannot be touched—those that are for one reason or another safe from being outsourced.

REVIEW QUESTIONS

1. Friedman makes the point emphatically that not only companies but also individual workers exist in a global environment. That is, workers today and increasingly in the future will compete globally for their jobs. Someone whose work is mediocre, who does not create value every day, is at risk of losing that job to energetic, creative workers overseas who can do the job better, at lower cost.

2. The "untouchables," according to Friedman, are those whose work cannot be "digitized, automated, or outsourced." Their work is "nonfungible," in the language of one CEO Friedman mentions. Anyone who wants a secure job, therefore, should gain the skill set to become an untouchable.

3. Friedman predicts that the new untouchables will fall into three categories: (1) specialists whose unique skills will keep them in demand in a global market; (2) "localized" or "anchored" workers who deliver goods and services in person, like a barber or neurosurgeon—see also Alan Blinder's "personal services" worker; and (3) provisionally nunfungible workers

26

(radiologists, accountants) who must quickly understand the pressures of the global economy on their work or risk losing their jobs to outsourcing.

4. A bell-curve economy has a large, stable middle class. A barbell economy has many rich, many poor, and a miniscule or non-existent middle class. Political stability in a democracy is based on a large, stable middle class. The implication is clear: finding good work in the coming decades is not only a matter of concern for individuals but also a matter of policy makers, economists, and others who understand that, without a stable middle, democracy itself "cannot be stable."

Will Your Job Be Exported? (p. 243)

ALAN S. BLINDER

The selection by Alan S. Blinder appears in Chapter 1 and is summarized in this chapter. In order to answer the following questions, students will have to reread this article which they've previously read in learning how to write summaries.

REVIEW QUESTIONS

1. In the global economy, producers of goods and services looking to lower costs of production "offshore" work by contracting with cheaper labor overseas. Offshoring is a well-known practice in the manufacturing sector. Until recently, service jobs were understood to require the presence of a person delivering the service. While this remains so for certain types of service providers (surgeons, for instance), it is not necessarily true for others (computer programmers). Advances in technology have made it possible for more and more service jobs to be offshored, or outsourced.

2. Blinder makes what he calls a "critical distinction" between personal services, which must be delivered on site by a worker, and impersonal services, which can be completed at a distance (without degrading the product) and delivered electronically. The distinction is important because impersonal service jobs are being offshored, just as manufacturing jobs have been for decades. Impersonal services (both high-end, like certain types of law and computer coding, and low-end, like call center staffing) are being delivered at a lower wage by trained workers overseas.

3. The amount of education workers had in the past was directly correlated to the quality and security of their jobs. Increasingly, educational preparation

27

will have little bearing on which jobs get offshored and which remain in the United States. The key determinant will be whether a service job is "personal" or "impersonal." (See question 2).

4. Blinder thinks the following advice (paragraph 17) would be appropriate: "Prepare yourself for a high-end personal service occupation that is not offshorable."

5. Blinder claims that offshoring will hit the service sector harder than the manufacturing sector for three reasons (paragraph 7). Service jobs "vastly" outnumber manufacturing jobs in the United States and other industrialized countries. Advances in technology will increase the range of service that can be delivered from a distance, electronically. And the skill of foreign workers "seems certain" to improve.

Into the Unknown (p. 244)

THE ECONOMIST

This article introduces the concept of "creative destruction"; that is, while the new economy is cutting many jobs, other jobs are being created. The article also discusses the outsourcing of many jobs, particularly in Information Technology (IT), but it also points out that in many areas the workplace is stable.

REVIEW QUESTIONS

1. See paragraph 3. The economy eliminates jobs as it automates, digitizes, and outsources them. Through these actions, businesses cut costs and lower prices, which in turn frees up money for both corporations and individuals to buy new goods and services. These new demands create opportunities for entrepreneurs, who create jobs (cf. the footnote for "creative destruction," p. 234).

2. Both former chairman of the Federal Reserve Bank Alan Greenspan and economist William Nordhaus claim that anxiety about future jobs is misplaced because "most of [these jobs] will involve producing goods and services that have not yet been invented" (paragraph 4). New technologies will make goods and services available that cannot yet be imagined. As this happens, workers will be needed to provide these goods and services.

3. Rule-bound and repetitive jobs are the most easily offshored—precisely the sort of jobs that have been lost in the past to automation. The opportunity created by the shedding of such jobs is that employers will "redeploy the workers concerned to jobs that create more value" (paragraph 12).

4. What some people desire, others provide—at a price. This is the dynamic that fuels the economy.

Occupational Outlook Handbook, 2008-09 Edition (p. 248)

BUREAU OF LABOR STATISTICS

The Bureau of Labor Statistics provides detailed information about key elements of hundreds of "Tomorrow's Jobs," information that students might be researching for their writing projects, or researching as they pursue their own employment.

REVIEW QUESTIONS

1. In the left column, a top-level menu under "OOH Home" lists broad categories of occupation: Management, Profession, Service, . . . Armed Forces." Linked in a second-level pull-down menu for most of these are associated job categories. Thus, associated with Service, OOH lists the general categories of Health Support, Protective Service, Food Preparation and Serving Related, Building and Grounds Cleaning and Maintenance, and Personal Care and Service. In turn, a third-level menu lists specific jobs associated with each job category. For Protective Service Occupations, OOH lists five specific jobs: Corrections officers, Fire fighting occupations, Police and detectives, Private detectives and investigators, and Security guards and gaming surveillance officers.

2. OOH presents nine date-rich categories of information for each specific job in its database (i.e., the third-level job listings—see #1 above). Following a brief bullet list of "Significant Points," information is presented in the following categories: Nature of the work; Training, other qualifications, and advancement; Employment; Job outlook; Projections date; Earnings; OES (Occupational Employment Statistics) data; Related occupations; and Sources of additional information.

3. The Occupational Employment Statistics (OES) page on the Bureau of Labor Statistics Web site "produces employment and wage estimates for over 800

29

occupations . . . These estimates are available for the nation as a whole, for individual states, and for metropolitan areas." Each occupation listed on an OES page has an identifying designation. For example, "aerospace engineers" is listed as 17-2011.

4. "Tomorrow's Jobs" is a BLS report that "presents highlights of Bureau of Labor Statistics' projections of the labor force and occupational and industry employment." The BLS provides these projections to "help guide [job seekers'] career plans."

5. "Tomorrow's Jobs" provides statistically based projections for changes occurring in the U.S. population, employment patterns, composition of the labor force, and other broad categories, providing bar-graph summaries of each.

6. Under the heading "Labor Force," for instance, we learn that "The youth labor force, aged 16 to 24, is expected to decrease its share of the labor force to 12.7 percent by 2016."

7. Under the "Industry" heading, we learn that the long-term trend from a goods-producing to a service-producing economy will continue. Healthcare and related occupations industries are expected to grow significantly, by 25.4 percent. Manufacturing, overall, is expected to decline by 10.6 percent.

Are They Really Ready to Work? (p. 250)

JILL CASNER-LOTTO and LINDA BARRINGTON

In this selection, Jill Casner-Lotto and Linda Barrington list and explain the reasons that businesses find recent high-school, two-year college, and four-year college graduates largely unready to meet the needs of the workplace.

REVIEW QUESTIONS

1. This report was commissioned by four organizations whose mission is to improve the competitiveness of American business. In the spring of 2006, The conference Board, Corporate Voices for Working Families, the Partnership for Twenty-First Century Skills, and the Society for Human Resource Management commissioned a survey of 400 human resource staff at 400 companies in order to learn what skills were needed by new entrants to the workforce and to assess the readiness of new entrants to take on the

30

work of the twenty-first-century global economy. The goal of the report was to sound a wake-up call to "the business community, educators, policy makers, students and their families"—to the people who have direct responsibility for preparing new entrants to the twenty-first-century workforce. Ultimately, the goal of the report is to help make American business and American workers competitive in the global economy.

2. Academic skills: the rudiments of speaking and reading; a functional knowledge of mathematics, science, government, economics, and the humanities; and so on. Applied skills: *using* basic knowledge in a work environment. Applied skills include the ability to think critically and solve problems, to speak and write effectively, to be a productive member of a team, to appreciate diversity, and to lead. Businesses see applied skills as more important than basic knowledge for all new entrants to the workforce. (See Tables 3-5 for details.)

3. Survey respondents identified four applied skills as "critical" or "important" for new entrants to the workforce: professionalism/work ethic, teamwork/collaboration, oral communication, and critical thinking/problem solving.

4. "[O]ne-quarter of four-year college graduates are perceived to be deficiently prepared in Written Communication." Ninety-three percent of survey respondents considered written English a very important skill for four-year college graduates.

5. Four-year college entrants were perceived to be excellent in the applied skill of Creativity/Innovation—good news in that business is driven by creativity and innovation.

6. The confluence of three trends makes the timing of this report particularly important. The dynamics of the global economy are creating an increasingly competitive business environment; much of the current workforce—the baby-boom generation—is retiring, placing demands on new entrants to be ready to fill positions; and the new economy demands workforce readiness for an increasingly complex technological business environment. These trends all highlight the need for a well-prepared workforce.

Engineering (p. 262)

RICHARD K. MILLER

According to Richard K. Miller, the changes in the field of engineering have been profound, so much so that an innovative college was founded to better prepare engineers for work in the twenty-first century. Many of the changes that have touched this field deal with non-technical areas: teamwork, communications skills, creative problem solving, and a strong sense of ethics, among others.

REVIEW QUESTIONS

1. Engineering changed significantly after the Cold War. Before and during the Cold War, the work of engineers was largely devoted to classified government projects that, for security reasons, eliminated the possibility of collaborating with others in different countries. With the federal government as their only client, engineers did not have to develop any business awareness. As well, engineers tended to work with others in their same specialty, limiting their exposure to other fields and ways of thinking about technical challenges. The end of the Cold War brought significant changes. Companies moved to new (and expensive) computer-based technologies that streamlined work; companies partnered with firms in Asia and Europe; partnering created a 24-hour workday, substantially reducing completion time for projects. Organizations that did not change suffered in the marketplace and some went out of business.

2. The major reforms emphasize communication skills; basic business awareness; and the ability to work in teams, with people from diverse cultures and experts outside the engineer's own specialty.

3. Engineers entering the workforce were overqualified technically: they possessed far more technical knowledge than they needed to complete their jobs. At the same time, they were "badly uneducated" in "the nature of business, and also the ability to communicate effectively with others." Young engineers also lacked experience with the design process and with manufacturing.

4. Advancement in a company depends not just on technical competence but also on communication skills—the key point of the industry leader Miller quotes at length. Communication skills, team building, leadership, and

32

business awareness all contribute to advancement through an organization. Ultimately, the ability to complete a job on budget and on time while "growing the business" marks a candidate for promotion.

5. Miller uses the examples of aerospace engineering and nuclear power to illustrate his point that unrecognized market and political considerations make predicting the future of jobs in the technology sector difficult at best. Rather than devoting themselves to the study of a "likely" hot technology in the future, Miller advises young engineers to pursue fascinating, inspiring topics of deep, personal interest. Students thus invested, who are "excellent at what they do," will be attractive to employers and will succeed.

Law (p. 268)

TOM MCGRATH

In this selection, Tom McGrath looks at the changes in the legal profession, changes which have nationwide repercussions. McGrath finds that being a good lawyer is no longer sufficient in a corporate world where the push for profits is all-consuming.

REVIEW QUESTIONS

1. According to McGrath, the profession of law has entered the "fast-moving" and "generally unforgiving twenty-first-century global economy" and is now subject to the technological and economic expectations of other businesses. As a consequence, law firms are opening offices around the country and world to service the global interests of clients. In addition, the *American Lawyer* Rankings, which lists salaries for attorneys at different firms, has contributed to the view of law as a business. Firms seek ever-higher compensation to maintain pay parity for attorneys and to attract new talent.

2. "Ennui" is weariness with life. An increasing number of lawyers, faced with the pressures of earning ever-greater amounts of money by billing more hours and "developing" clients (finding new clients who can pay the billable rate), are feeling that their practice "can suck the soul out of you." Law formerly had been regarded as a profession in which practitioners expert in the law served the needs of clients "in the courtroom or boardroom" (paragraph 14). Today, the profession is so focused on money that the initial motivation for entering the profession may be lost.

3. Other professionals earn money through "economies of scale" or by "taking a percentage of a deal or the cost of a project." Lawyers earn money through billable hours: that is, they sell their time. Because a lawyer's time is finite, so, too, is the money they can make. "To compensate for that labor-intensive business model," firms squeeze as much work out of young associates as possible—sometimes as much as 90 hours a week. Driven by the profit motive, firms may shed parts of their practice that do not earn enough money or "de-equitize" partners (that is, strip them of their status as profit-sharing partners and demote them to salaried employees).

Medicine (p. 271)

MATT RICHTEL

In this selection, Matt Richtel explains how specialties in medicine have changed as prospective doctors, especially women, choose areas of specialty that will allow them to put in as normal a work week as possible. For these doctors, a manageable lifestyle is more important than huge income.

REVIEW QUESTIONS

1. Observers have noted a steep decline in particularly labor-intensive specialties such as family practice, which require long work weeks and erratic hours. At the same time, specialties with predictable schedules are in greater demand. For example, there has been "a 40 percent increase in students pursuing [dermatology] over the last five years, compared with a 40 percent drop in those interested in family practice."

2. The most sought-after specialties—like dermatology, anesthesiology, and radiology—offer the practicing physician a predictable 40-55 hour/week schedule, unlike family practice and surgery, which may require many more hours per week and which require responses to emergency calls during nights and weekends.

3. See paragraph 7. "Lifestyle" considerably outweighs "income" as a criterion for selecting a specialty—55 percent to 9 percent. The importance of lifestyle over income has created a "brain drain": the brightest students are rejecting specialties like surgery and family practice in favor of professions like radiology and dermatology that offer a lighter, more regular work schedule.

4. Women who want families want dependable schedules that leave time for family life. Not only does dermatology, for instance, offer a family-friendly schedule (with few if any emergency calls during nights or weekends), it also pays more than specialties like family practice or pediatrics. As a result, more women (and men) physicians who want a regular schedule are choosing specialties like dermatology.

VIDEO LINKS

A Changing Landscape

> The New World of Work (Statistics set to music)
> http://www.youtube.com/watch?v=oL6GTqvtYHM&NR=1
>
> Managing Tomorrow's People (Video / PriceWaterhouseCoopers report)
> http://www.pwc.co.uk/eng/issues/
> managing_tomorrows_people_the_future_of_work_to_2020.html
>
> The Future of Work [in Business] (Talk by MIT Professor Thomas W. Malone)
> http://mitworld.mit.edu/video/229

The New Workplace

> No Office (ABC News Report)
> http://www.youtube.com/watch?v=ZmfXksLir1g
>
> Workers in Waiting (Technology and social interaction, British)
> http://www.youtube.com/watch?v=ZCVxsgFZJBU
>
> Office of the Future (Virtual reality, comic skit)
> http://www.youtube.com/
> watch?v=G_jMGApsAnM&feature=related

Multiple Generations in the Modern Workplace

> Generation Next in the Workplace
> http://www.youtube.com/watch?v=y_jB1Q0K5BI&feature=related

Generations in the Workplace 2007
http://www.youtube.com/watch?v=-f6XxWr7DUo&feature=related

Outsourcing

The Other Side of Outsourcing (with Thomas Friedman)
http://www.youtube.com/watch?v=8quDb3FIUuo

ABC News: Myth: Outsourcing Bad for America
http://www.youtube.com/watch?v=A2IRrfcvVCg&feature=related

ABC News Report on Outsourcing (Part 1)
http://www.youtube.com/watch?v=FwwgXCOEYks&feature=related

ABC News Report on Outsourcing (Part 2)
http://www.youtube.com/watch?v=tXulLCkDf8Q&feature=related

Outsource This (skit with Jason Alexander)
http://www.youtube.com/watch?v=uIiwrPFQQq8&feature=related

Tom Peters, Management consultant

People in China Starving for Your Job
http://www.youtube.com/watch?v=aOxxBvmpbZU

Educate for a Creative Society
http://www.youtube.com/watch?v=h_w4AfflmeM

Chapter 8

Green Power

The reading selections in this chapter fall into two broad categories: first, the general challenges presented by global warming, and, second, the use of renewable energy resources in combating the problem of global warming. Michael D. Lemonick's article opens the chapter in discussing the rise of temperatures around the globe. Thomas L. Friedman then points out the superficiality of many "green solutions," while showing that the planet's condition continues to worsen. Next, Al Gore, Nobel Peace Prize winner for his environmental activism, outlines the problems inherent in our dependency on foreign oil and proposes that we move away from such dependence to rely on renewable energy sources. In contrast, Robert Bryce argues that such freedom from reliance on foreign energy sources is impossible. The Report of an Independent Task Force by the Council on Foreign Relations examines the implications of the country's dependence on oil and makes recommendations to decrease this dependence. Mindy S. Lubber reports on the financial implications to investors and corporations of ignoring the impact of the carbon footprints created by corporations. The first part of this chapter concludes with Mortimer B. Zuckerman, who recommends a number of measures to reduce our dependence on foreign oil.

The second part of the chapter opens with Don Sherman's examination of the readiness of General Motors to go green with the Chevy Volt. Next, Joseph, B. White argues that the gasoline-powered internal combustion engine still has a long life ahead of it. Michael Totty then presents both sides of the debate about nuclear power. This is followed by Elizabeth Kolbert's report on the successful conversion to wind power by an entire Danish island and Sterling Burnett's discussion of the negative side of wind power. Marla Dickerson discusses California's push to end dependence on sources of energy from outside the state. At the end of the chapter, Peter Maloney reports on "Environmentalists Against Solar Power."

The Internet offers a wealth of material on the subject of climate change and green power. A list of video links on "Green Power" concludes the chapter. Included are several links to videos regarding wind power and nuclear power.

Also offered is an NBC Report on the Chevrolet Volt (G.M.'s new electric car) that would make a good companion piece to Sherman's selection.

Global Warming: Beyond the Tipping Point (p. 284)

MICHAEL D. LEMONICK

As the title of this selection indicates, there is real concern among many scientists that unless immediate and widespread action is taken to decrease the amount of carbon in the earth's atmosphere, catastrophic changes could ensue. But Lemonick also reports that not all scientists share Hansen's conclusions.

REVIEW QUESTIONS

1. Hansen and his colleagues conclude that unless carbon emissions are reduced, the global mean temperature is likely to rise by the end of the twenty-first century by 6 degrees Celsius, enough to trigger major climatic disruption. They assert that to prevent such climatic catastrophe, we need to reduce current CO_2 levels to no more than 350 ppm (parts per million).

2. The burning of fossil fuels such as coal, oil, and natural gas generates CO_2 and other greenhouse gases. During the daytime CO_2 allows the sun to shine through to heat the earth's surface, but at night it traps the infrared rays that the earth radiates into space in the atmosphere. Over time, the trapped heat increases the temperature of the oceans and the atmosphere, causing global warming.

3. The Charney sensitivity "estimates how much the global mean temperature will rise if atmospheric CO_2 is doubled from its preindustrial levels." It does not take into account climate feedback mechanisms (such as changes in water vapor) and it assumes no changes in such long term factors such as changes in glaciation and the ocean's ability to absorb CO_2.

4. The melting of huge masses of ice and glaciers in Greenland and West Antarctica will also increase dark land mass, which will, in turn, absorb greater quantities of the solar radiation, contributing to global warming. It will also raise ocean levels, affecting other parts of the globe, particularly coastal regions.

5. Some experts, while concerned about climate changes, are less alarmed than Hansen and his colleagues because they say that the mechanisms of global

38

warming—including climate sensitivity and feedback mechanisms—are not fully understood. They also question the accuracy and meaning of some of Hansen's "absolute" numbers, particularly the estimated increases in global temperature.

6. Hansen and his colleagues recommend: (1) that all future industrial plants be equipped with technology to capture CO_2 and that existing plants be retrofitted with this capability; (2) that large areas that have been cleared of trees—which absorb CO_2—be reforested.

205 Easy Ways to Save the Earth (p. 290)

THOMAS L. FRIEDMAN

Thomas L. Friedman says that the minor, everyday efforts of the average consumer to "go green" are entirely insufficient to halt global warming. What is needed is mammoth, worldwide effort to make essential changes regarding such things as deforestation, transportation, and dependence on fossil fuels.

REVIEW QUESTIONS

1. Friedman does not take seriously any effort to "save the earth" where no one gets hurt because only "symbolic gestures" are involved like changing to lower wattage light bulbs; which doesn't involve serious cost and sacrifice; or which doesn't involve massive effort on the part of both business and government.

2. Instead of a "green hallucination," Friedman asserts, we should be having "green revolution."

3. The scale problem indicates the degree to which the fossil fuel-based transportation system would have to be shut down, reduced in size, or replaced with alternative energy vehicles in order to create a significant reduction in total carbon emissions. Devices that use alternative forms of energy would need to be built and deployed in massive quantities, more massive than anything being considered over the next few years. The occasional rooftop solar panel, small-scale wind farm, or hybrid vehicle won't make a noticeable difference.

4. Socolow and Pacala's 25-wedge pie chart was designed to illustrate the enormity of the task of significantly reducing global carbon emissions. Each

39

wedge represents the reduction over the next fifty years of 25 billion tons of carbon emissions. Among the wedges: "Double fuel efficiency of two billion cars from 30 miles per gallon to 60 mpg"; "Increase solar power seven-hundred fold to displace all coal-fired power"; "Halt all cutting and burning of forests." As Friedman notes, "If the world managed to take just one of those steps, it would be a miracle. Eight would be the miracle of miracles, but this is the scale of what will be required." But according to Socolow and Pacala, eight of these wedges would have to be deployed to avoid doubling the levels of CO_2 in the atmosphere by 2050.

5. With their huge sizes and populations, China and India are the developing nations whose accelerating economic growth will likely involve doubling or tripling their current levels of carbon emissions; these countries, along with the United States, pose the greatest threat to the stability of global climate.

The Climate for Change (p. 302)

AL GORE

Like Friedman, Al Gore calls for reducing our dependence on fossil fuels and for an end to deforestation. He also connects the environmental crisis to other challenges we face, particularly in the areas of economics and national security. He concludes by proposing a five-part plan to "repower America."

REVIEW QUESTIONS

1. Gore argues that massive investment in alternative energy technology is the best way to create new jobs that will bolster the nation's economy. Moreover, we increase our national security by reducing our dependence upon Middle Eastern oil; and we save billions of dollars that would otherwise be sent abroad.

2. Gore calls the nation to commit itself to "producing 100 percent of our electricity from carbon-free sources within ten years."

3. Responses will vary, but students should mention (1) constructing wind and solar farms; (2) planning and constructing a "smart grid" to transport electricity from the rural areas where it is generated to cities; (3) converting the American auto industry from internal combustion engines to plug-in hybrids; (4) retrofitting buildings to make them better insulated and more

energy efficient; (5) levying a carbon tax and working to place limits on carbon dioxide throughout the world; and working to reduce deforestation.

The Dangerous Delusions of Energy Independence (p. 305)

ROBERT BRYCE

While the call for energy independence grows, Robert Bryce argues that such independence is just not possible in the near future and that Americans are "woefully ignorant" regarding the economic and political aspects of the issue.

REVIEW QUESTIONS

1. Bryce notes that "America's self-image is inextricably bound to the concepts of freedom and autonomy." Thus, the Declaration of Independence's promise of life, liberty, and the pursuit of happiness is a component of our national DNA.

2. Bryce believes that renewable energy sources such as wind and solar power cannot replace fossil fuels for the foreseeable future because, at least for the next 30 to 50 years, they cannot be supplied on a sufficient scale to satisfy the nation's ever-increasing energy requirements. We will therefore be energy interdependent with the rest of the world—and particularly, with the Middle East—for many years to come.

3. Bryce asserts that the American public, besides being obsessed with independence, "is woefully ignorant about the fundamentals of the energy business." Energy independence, he argues, is a politically acceptable cover for foreign policy isolationism, protectionist trade policies, and support of domestic energy producers such as the corn ethanol industry.

National Security Consequences of U.S. Oil Dependence (p. 312)

REPORT OF AN INDEPENDENT TASK FORCE OF THE COUNCIL ON FOREIGN RELATIONS

This report underscores some of Bryce's ideas, especially that we will continue to depend on foreign oil and that an understanding of energy markets is essential. The report makes a number of recommendations regarding the lessening of our dependence on foreign oil and the need to increase production of domestic oil, at least in the short term.

There are no Review Questions for this report.

Balance Sheets and the Climate Crisis: How American Businesses Can Help (p. 316)

MINDY S. LUBBER

Mindy S. Lubber moves the discussion from science and politics to business and finance. She discusses global warming as "a significant, material risk to our financial markets" and argues that, along with the government, business must play a major role in addressing the problem of global climate change and promoting energy efficiency. In doing so, she says, business must forgo short-term profits and seek solutions that will, over the long term, prove economically profitable.

There are no Review Questions for this selection.

Stop the Energy Insanity (p. 323)

MORTIMER B. ZUCKERMAN

Businessman and publisher Mortimer B. Zuckerman argues that in order to decrease our dependence on foreign oil and address the high cost of fuel the United States should increase domestic oil production and exploration. He also points out the cost-effectiveness and energy-effectiveness of rail transport versus the use of cars and trucks.

REVIEW QUESTIONS

1. Responses will vary; but students should cover Zuckerman's recommendations for increased oil production and exploration; reducing barriers to building or expanding new oil refineries; increasing research and development support for more energy efficient power plants; fixing our mass transit system; raising fuel economy standards; increasing the gas tax; and pursuing alternative energy technologies.

2. Zuckerman points out that there were no oil spills even during Hurricanes Katrina and Rita, which destroyed oil platforms in the Gulf of Mexico. Nor have there been oil spills from offshore drilling activities in the offshore regions of the Scandinavian countries, the Netherlands, and Great Britain. The greatest oil spills, he points out, result from leaking oil tankers.

3. Rail mass transit is about 10 times more efficient than road transit because of economies of scale: "A single locomotive run by two men can haul the same amount of freight as 70 modern semitrailer truck rigs with 70 drivers. One passenger train can take 1000 cars off the road."

G.M. at 100: Is Its Future Electric? (p. 327)

DON SHERMAN

Often a leader in developing new automotive technologies, General Motors promises that its Volt will not only be "green" but affordable. While the car is much anticipated, there is some doubt as to whether the car can deliver on G.M.'s promises. One problem, Don Sherman points out, is the cost of the lithium-ion battery on which the car's propulsion depends; another is the life of the battery.

REVIEW QUESTIONS

1. After several years, G.M. re-possessed all EV1s and destroyed them. The chief problem of this all-electric vehicle was its limited range—only about 50 miles on a single charge.

2. Unlike the EV1, the Volt has a backup power system: a gasoline engine, drawing on a 12-gallon gas tank which powers a generator that supplies electric current to the battery pack and the vehicle's drive motor. The backup power increases the range of the Volt from about 40 miles on a single battery charge to about 400 miles. Still, the chief drawbacks of the Volt remain the limits and cost of the battery. G.M. engineers must improve the battery to increase its driving range on a single charge and also to make the car appealing to the mass market by reducing the battery cost below $10,000.

3. The Volt is not considered a conventional hybrid because the electric motor is its only propulsion source. The onboard gasoline engine sends power only to the generator and to the electric motor. It does not, like a conventional gas engine, supply power through a transmission system to the drive shaft.

Why the Gasoline Engine Isn't Going Away Any Time Soon (p. 332)

JOSEPH B. WHITE

Journalist Joseph B. White, whose beat includes energy and automobiles, argues that because major change is best done incrementally, the life of the internal-combustion engine is far from over. Major reasons for its longevity and popularity are its relatively low cost when measured against the cost of hybrids, its familiarity, and its proven track record.

REVIEW QUESTIONS

1. Responses will vary but should include references to (1) the incremental nature of technological change; (2) the fact that the internal-combustion engine is "integral to modern life," particularly the fact that so much of the population lives in the suburbs; (3) improvements in efficiency of internal-combustion engines, making alternative technologies less desirable; (4) the costs of dismantling existing auto plants and dismissing their workers, as well as the costs of building a new infrastructure to distribute alternative fuels.

2. Internal-combustion engines may be bad for the environment, but they also have advantages that many consumers would be loath to give up: "low cost, durability and power." They also allow people to live long distances from where they work; our modern suburban lifestyle is dependent upon the gasoline-powered automobile.

3. Hydrogen and natural gas are more difficult than gasoline and diesel to transport and store. There is at present no national infrastructure that would allow vehicles powered by hydrogen and natural gas to easily re-fuel.

The Case For and Against Nuclear Power (p. 339)

MICHAEL TOTTY

In this *Wall Street Journal* article Michael Totty presents both sides of the argument regarding nuclear power. On the positive side, Totty points out that nuclear power plants do not contribute to global warming and can be more safely built than they were in the past. On the other hand, nuclear power plants pose huge problems, not least among them how and where to store nuclear waste.

REVIEW QUESTIONS

1. Nuclear power plants emit virtually no carbon dioxide or other greenhouse gases and thus do not contribute to global warming.

2. Responses will vary, but students should note the high cost of building nuclear power plants; the regulatory hurdles; safety concerns (e.g., leakage of

44

radioactive emissions into the atmosphere, the "China Syndrome"); the technical and political problems of disposing of nuclear waste; and the threat of nuclear proliferation caused by diversion or theft of enriched uranium for use in bombs.

3. Newer nuclear plants are considered safer than old ones because the more recent reactors are housed within reinforced concrete structures up to four feet thick. They also incorporate safer pump and piping systems for cooling the hot nuclear core.

4. Responses will vary. Assuming the primary headings to be "I. Costs; II. Safety; III. Nuclear Proliferation," each primary heading will incorporate subheadings of "A. Pro; B. Con," followed by Arabic number subcategories for points covered by Totty. For example, under I.A, students could note that 1, costs of plants will decline as more are built; 2. government may provide loan guarantees and other federal incentives to support plant construction.

The Island in the Wind (p. 347)

ELIZABETH KOLBERT

Journalist Elizabeth Kolbert, whose specialty is environmentalism, here reports on the Danish island of Samsø which now draws all of its electrical energy from wind power. In addition to harnessing wind power, Samsingers have instituted other means of drawing down their carbon footprint. All of this was accomplished in about a decade and offers a glimpse of what may be possible in a world facing serious disruptions because of climate change. But can Samsø's achievement be duplicated in other demographically different regions?

REVIEW QUESTIONS

1. The focal sentences making the connection between Samsø's experience with wind power and global CO_2 emissions occur in paragraph 11: "Samsø transformed its energy systems in a single decade. Its experience suggests how the carbon problem, as huge as it is, could be dealt with, if we were willing to try."

2. On the island of Samsø, notes Kolbert, "the wind of the Kattegat [an arm of the North Sea where Samsø is located] blows pretty much continuously," so the wind turbines are almost always turning.

45

3. Kolbert notes that "while fossil fuels release carbon that would otherwise have remained sequestered, biomass releases carbon that would have entered the atmosphere anyway. As long as biomass regrows, the CO_2 released in its combustion should be reabsorbed, meaning that the cycle is—or at least can be—carbon neutral."

Wind Power Puffery (p. 355)

H. STERLING BURNETT

In this op-ed Sterling Burnett itemizes some of the objections to the use of wind-generated power, among them the obvious one—that wind farms can generate energy only when the wind is blowing. But there are other drawbacks to tall wind turbines besides that one, says Burnett: the damage to bird and bat species and, in some areas, their growing unpopularity.

There are no review questions for this selection.

State Solar Plans Are as Big as All Outdoors (p. 358)

MARLA DICKERSON

Los Angeles Times writer Marla Dickerson here reports on solar power, especially as it is being adopted in California's move toward energy self-sufficiency. Dickerson also points out some of the challenges in creating cost-effective solar energy systems large enough to power entire communities.

REVIEW QUESTIONS

1. Size matters in solar power because only large-scale solar farms (as opposed to individual rooftop solar panels installed at the discretion of individual homeowners or individual companies) can generate sufficient power to meet the nation's energy needs.

2. Disadvantages of large-scale solar farms: they require large tracts of land; the power generated must still be transmitted over old-fashioned electrical towers and high-voltage lines; they threaten fragile ecosystems; and they mar the beauty of the landscape on which they are built.

3. Recent state laws in California have mandated that a significant percentage of the state's power must be generated from renewable sources and that greenhouse gas emissions must be significantly reduced.

46

Environmentalists Against Solar Power (p. 362)

PETER MALONEY

As his title indicates, Peter Maloney here outlines the arguments against solar power systems including cost and the problems associated with the protection of—or the loss of—ecosystems and endangered species.

REVIEW QUESTIONS

1. Responses will vary: students' summaries should cover environmentalists' objections to large scale solar power arrays obstructing scenic views; disturbing wildlife habitats, including those of endangered species; and drawing for their operation from the state's limited water supply.

2. Feed-in tariffs, used in Germany, offer "fixed-rate payments for electricity generated from solar panels" and thus provide financial incentives for homeowners to install rooftop solar panels.

3. The rooftop solar panels favored by some environmentalists pose few or none of the drawbacks mentioned above (response to Review Question #1), but the power generated is not sufficient to replace more than a small fraction of the energy generated by conventional coal-fired electrical plants: "At the current rate of adding 200 megawatts of rooftop solar power a year, it would take 100 years to meet the 20% renewable target that California must meet by 2010."

VIDEO LINKS

Climate Change

> Climate Change (AAAS: American Association for the Advancement of Science)
> http://www.youtube.com/watch?v=_nZjrPoAlbU

> Frontline: "Heat" (trailer for PBS program on climate change)
> http://www.youtube.com/watch?v=5ZhZVYYpQYo

> Climate Change (British perspective: climatechallenge.gov.uk)
> http://www.youtube.com/watch?v=zzjOcOcQ90U

Al Gore Goes Green for "An Inconvenient Truth"
http://www.youtube.com/watch?v=sHcEj92QtB8

Solar Power 101: How Does Sunlight Turn into Electricity?
(Sierra Solar Systems)
http://www.youtube.com/watch?v=DFDn6eTV0jQ

Solar Power Breakthrough? (www.worldsnest.com)
http://www.youtube.com/watch?v=7_Ctw3zA2F4

"Wind Power" (National Agricultural Report)
http://www.youtube.com/watch?v=IcuWzTw_05M

Rooftop Wind Turbine—Perth, Australia
http://www.youtube.com/watch?v=WZ5kX5Yw4eY

Wind Power in Calgary, Canada
http://www.youtube.com/watch?v=Hg9fiDUroo4

Nuclear Power: How it Works (Ontario Power Generation)
http://www.youtube.com/watch?v=fjgdgAhOzXQ

Nuclear Power Station (animated graphic)
http://www.youtube.com/watch?v=igf96TS3Els

Nuclear Power Generator (live action and animation)
http://www.youtube.com/watch?v=VrhzkoNU84g&feature=related

Nuclear Energy (debate over nuclear power in Australia)
http://www.youtube.com/watch?v=-TB8pGY0GxI&feature=related

YouTube Debate (Democratic Presidential Candidates): Nuclear
Power?"
http://www.youtube.com/watch?v=XdMHHIO5tQM

Who Killed the Electric Car? (movie trailer)
http://www.youtube.com/watch?v=nsJAlrYjGz8

Electric Car: Bye Bye, Petroleum {WGN TV news report)
http://www.youtube.com/watch?v=PY8I_gyACvA&feature=PlayList&p
=3609339965AA7C3D&playnext=1&index=43

The Chevrolet Volt (NBC Report)
http://www.youtube.com/watch?v=wR7k1OlMXHk

The Unveiling of the Tesla Motors Electric Car
http://www.youtube.com/watch?v=hOl_1S10jTk

Chapter 9

Marriage and Family in America

This chapter offers reading selections that examine marriage and families from a wide range of perspectives, from major sociological studies to first-person narratives, including the current debate over gay marriage, the impact of mothers working outside the home—and the impact of not working outside the home—as well as a short story that offers a wry look at love and marriage.

The chapter opens with historian Stephanie Coontz's "pop quiz" on marriage, followed by a book chapter, "The Radical Idea of Marrying for Love." Next, David Popenoe and Barbara Dafoe Whitehead, co-directors of the National Marriage Project at Rutgers-The State University of New Jersey, provide a report card on the contemporary state of marriage. This is followed by opposing arguments on gay marriage, with writer Andrew Sullivan in favor of gay marriage and cultural conservative William J. Bennett against it.

Three authors then give more personal perspectives on marriage based on their own experiences. First, Terry Martin Hekker discusses, in two op-eds more than a quarter of a century apart, how her advocacy of the role of traditional homemaker underwent change. Two more op-eds, by Leslie Bennetts and Deborah Tannen, further the discussion of women's traditional roles and responsibilities.

In "American Marriage in Transition, sociologist Andrew J. Cherlin discusses two profound changes that occurred in marriage in the second half of the twentieth century. And Hope Edelman and Eric Bartels discuss the tensions and anger over housework that affect marriages. These selections are followed by Aviva Patz who asks "Will Your Marriage Last?" The chapter ends with a short story by Lore Segal.

The subject of marriage and family, while being studied by historians, sociologists and others, often invites impassioned commentary from non-researchers. Some of the breadth of information and opinion on the Web is available in the video links at the end of this chapter. Of particular note might be the "Love and Marriage in Modern America" with Stephanie Coontz as a guest and the Charlie Rose 1996 panel discussion on gay marriage which includes Andrew Sullivan as a panelist.

A Pop Quiz on Marriage: The Radical Idea of Marrying for Love (p. 378)

STEPHANIE COONTZ

So closely is marriage associated with romance in contemporary culture that students may be surprised to learn that marrying for love is really a fairly recent idea with its roots in the Enlightenment. Stephanie Coontz provides important historical and cultural perspectives on marriage as we understand it today.

REVIEW QUESTIONS

1. Two major social changes in the eighteenth century helped bring about a new view of the relationship between love and marriage in western civilization: (1) the spread of wage labor made prospective husbands less dependent upon long apprenticeships and both partners less dependent upon financial help or bequests from their parents; (2) the intellectual ideas of the Enlightenment "championed individual rights," placed marital relationships on a more equal footing than in the past, and enhanced the value of love in marriage.

2. By placing love foremost in marriage, and therefore reducing the cynicism bred by marriage for money or property, those championing the "love match" model of marriage hoped to make the institution more secure.

3. The purpose of marriage, according to the writer, was to get people "to discharge the duties of civil society, to govern their families with prudence, and to educate their children with discretion."

4. Critics of the "love match" feared that two values—(1) free choice and (2) egalitarianism—could lead to individualism. For the examples, responses will vary. A feared consequence of free choice was that people would choose their mates unwisely. A feared consequence of egalitarianism was that men would not support their wives and families if they no longer had control over them—specifically over their labor.

The State of Our Unions (p. 392)

DAVID POPENOE AND BARBARA DAFOE WHITEHEAD

This selection combines sections of Popenoe and Whitehead's 2002 and 2005 reports on marriage. The authors are codirectors of the National Marriage Project at Rutgers, The State University of New Jersey. According to the authors, Americans have become less and less likely to marry. However, Popenoe and Whitehead also provide data on the risk factors for divorce and challenge claims that those who live together before marriage (i.e., "unmarried cohabitation") are more likely to face divorce. Additional information explores the economic implications of one's marriage status.

REVIEW QUESTIONS

1. Popenoe and Whitehead point out that "if you are a reasonably well-educated person with a decent income, come from an intact family and are religious, marry after age twenty-five without having a baby first, your chances of divorce are very low indeed."

2. Popenoe and Whitehead attribute the slight decline in divorce rate from the early 1980s to two probable reasons: "an increase in the age at which people marry for the first time, and a higher educational level of those marrying, both of which are associated with greater marital stability."

3. The higher percentage of divorced females is attributed by Popenoe and Whitehead primarily to the fact that divorced men are more likely to remarry than divorced women. They also point out that "among those who do remarry, men generally do so sooner than women."

4. According to Popenoe and Whitehead, this conclusion may be erroneous because it may reflect what they term the "selection effect"—meaning that those who cohabit before marriage have certain characteristics as opposed to those who do not, "and that it may be these characteristics, and not the experience of cohabitation, that lead to marital instability."

A Debate on Gay Marriage

For Gay Marriage (p. 406)

ANDREW SULLIVAN

In this article, Andrew Sullivan, a former editor of the *New Republic* magazine and a current editor of *The Atlantic*, argues that marriage is more than a private relationship between two people; it is also a public institution that must be available to everyone. He contends that as such, conservatives should support gay marriage rather than domestic partnerships since marriage is a stabilizing institution.

REVIEW QUESTIONS

1. According to Sullivan, "marriage has become a way in which the state recognizes an emotional commitment by two people to each other for life." Under that definition, marriage cannot be denied to homosexuals, "if one believes in equal rights under the law."

2. Sullivan indicates that minors (marrying one another or an adult) and close family relatives are two classes of people who cannot fulfill the marriage contract.

3. Responses will vary, but a sample response follows: "Sullivan believes that conservatives should favor gay marriage because (1) marriage assures equal protection of the laws, and (2) marriage fosters commitment and stability in couples' relationships and (3) provides role models for children. Conservatives should also favor gay marriage because the 'domestic partnership' concept could cause potential problems with litigation and subjective judicial decision-making, as well as damage the traditional prestige of marriage and undermine its legal advantages."

4. Sullivan argues that gay marriage will bridge the gulf often found between homosexuals and their parents by allowing the gay couple to join the family in a way that both the family and the couple can easily acknowledge.

Against Gay Marriage (p. 411)

WILLIAM J. BENNETT

William J. Bennett, former chairman of the National Endowment for the Humanities, secretary of education under President Reagan and President H. W. Bush's "drug czar," has also served as editor of the *National Review*. In his argument against gay marriage, he responds to Sullivan's points.

REVIEW QUESTIONS

1. The intelligent and shrewd conservative argument for gay marriage, according to Bennett, is that it will promote faithfulness and monogamy.

2. According to Bennett, if gay marriage is recognized, the sex education curriculum of schools will have to teach that heterosexual marriage and homosexual marriage are equivalent, thus putting parents who wish their children to be taught the "privileged status of heterosexual marriage" at odds with the new curriculum.

3. A possible response: "Bennett opposes broadening the definition of marriage to include same-sex unions because attempts to further broaden the definition to include other groups—such as brothers or bigamists—would surely follow, and because the definition of marriage as between a man and a woman reflects the wisdom of the ages and the teachings of all major religions."

The Satisfactions of Housewifery and Motherhood/Paradise Lost (Domestic Division) (p. 414)

TERRY MARTIN HEKKER

These two op-eds provide a look at a quandary facing today's mothers as Terry Martin Hekker, writing as a housewife in 1970, defends her decision to be a stay-at-home mother at a time when many women were choosing to join the workforce and then revisits her decision in 2006, when, after a shattering divorce ending 40 years of marriage, and not having worked outside the home, she finds herself unprepared to face financial responsibilities on her own.

There are no review questions for this reading.

A Mother's Day Kiss-Off (p. 420)

LESLIE BENNETTS

In this op-ed, Leslie Bennetts explores some of the ideas raised by Hekker, particularly those having to do with the realities faced by women who choose to be homemakers. For married women who have children and work outside the home, Bennetts discusses the inequalities between men and women in balancing childcare and housework with work outside the home.

There are no review questions for this reading.

Understanding Mom (p. 424)

DEBORAH TANNEN

In an op-ed, published opposite the one above by Bennetts, Deborah Tannen discusses the gulf between the choice her mother made to be a homemaker and the choice Tannen has made to do just the opposite. Tannen describes the difficulty she and her mother have in trying to understand the choices each of them has made.

There are no review questions for this reading.

American Marriage in Transition (p. 426)

ANDREW J. CHERLIN

Sociologist Andrew J. Cherlin reports on "Two Transitions in the Meaning of Marriage" which are "the result of long-term cultural and material trends that altered the meaning of marriage during the twentieth century." Marriage has changed, according to Cherlin, in significant personal and social ways even while it has continued to be important symbolically.

REVIEW QUESTIONS

1. Changing practices in the division of labor between marriage partners, along with the increasing rate of childbearing outside of marriage contributed to the "deinstitutionalization" or marriage.

2. The *institutional marriage* was characterized by a set of social norms that allowed each partner to fulfill her or his role such as the "good parent or the loyal and supportive spouse." During the 1950s, the institutional marriage

55

evolved into the *companionate marriage*, in which the marriage partners "were supposed to be each other's companions—friends, lovers—to an extent not imagined by spouses in the institutional marriages of the previous era." Emotional satisfaction was key to the success of the companionate marriage. During this era, marriage was the only acceptable social framework for having sexual relationships and children. In the following two decades, however, companionate marriage gave way to *individualized marriage*, characterized by an emphasis on self-development and self-expression, flexibility of roles within marriage, and communication and openness in confronting problems.

3. Contemporary marriages, Cherlin believes, are characterized by (1) a high degree of *choice* (whether or not to get married, when to get married, whether to have children outside of or within marriage, whether to marry someone of the same gender, how to allocate the tasks associated with childcare and housework); and (2) a change in the types of *rewards* that marriage partners seek (personal choice and growth, self-development, intimacy, open communication).

The Myth of Co-Parenting: How It Was Supposed to Be. How It Was. (p. 431)

HOPE EDELMAN

In this selection, Hope Edelman details the anger and sense of hopelessness that she felt after the birth of her first child at the same time that her husband was starting a new business, a situation that pushed her out of her job and made her a full-time homemaker.

There are no review questions for this selection.

My Problem with Her Anger (p. 438)

ERIC BARTELS

Eric Bartels describes the quandary of being on the receiving end of his wife's anger over housework and childcare.

There are no review questions for this selection.

Will Your Marriage Last? (p. 445)

AVIVA PATZ

In reporting on the results of the PAIR Project, Aviva Patz, executive editor of *Psychology Today,* reports on a project study which found that what is usually thought of as the major reason for divorce—arguing and bickering—turns out to be much less important in predicting marital longevity than loss of love and affection.

REVIEW QUESTIONS

1. The purpose of the PAIR (Process of Adaptation in Intimate Relationships) Project was to identify predictors of success in marriage. Investigators followed 168 couples from Pennsylvania from their wedding day through the first 13 years of their marriage. The chief findings: (1) many newlyweds do not begin their marriage in blissful love: (2) those couples who do begin in blissful love are more likely to divorce because they cannot maintain such intensity of romantic feeling; (3) couples with less fulfilling marriages are less likely to divorce because there is less erosion of romance than is the case for the blissful couples; (4) the major cause of divorce for all couples is the loss of love and affection, and not the degree of argument and bickering that characterizes the marriage.

2. The first two years of marriage are critical, Ted Huston found. If the intensity of love and affection between the partners changes significantly during this period, the marriage is likely in trouble. If there is little or no change, the marriage is likely to succeed.

3. In many cases, traditional marriage counseling focuses on ways of managing or resolving conflict between the marital partners. The results of Huston's study suggest that a better focus might be in maintaining the intimacy and positive feelings toward one another that the couple enjoyed as newlyweds.

4. In the enduring dynamics model of marriage, "partners establish patterns of behavior early and maintain them over time"; it is a model that "highlights stability in the relationship" and thus tends to ensure marital success and endurance.

The Arbus Factor (p. 452)

LORE SEGAL

The title of Lore Segal's short story give a clue as to what readers might expect. "Arbus" refers to Diane Arbus, famous for her photographs of unorthodox subjects, images that force the viewer to rethink what the photographer has captured on film. Lore Segal's story does the same: it forces the reader to reconsider assumptions about love, marriage, and growing old.

There are no review questions for this selection.

VIDEO LINKS

Marriage in America

"Love and Marriage in Modern America": Host Peter Robinson, with guests Stephanie Coontz and Jennifer Roback Morse ("Uncommon Knowledge": Hoover Institution)
http://www.youtube.com/watch?v=3RK5iMHV53M

Charlie Rose: 1996 Panel Discussion on Gay Marriage, with Andrew Sullivan, Bobby Knight, Evan Wolfson, Robert George (starts at minute 38:10 of program)
http://www.charlierose.com/view/interview/6294

The Berkeley Symposium on Same Sex Marriage: Law and Politics
http://www.youtube.com/watch?v=EF6ALwBHz8U

"Why Gay Marriage is Wrong" (ironic)
http://www.youtube.com/watch?v=WYPVISQR9fY

Wanda Sykes on Gay Marriage (stand-up comedy routine)
http://www.youtube.com/watch?v=R4oGKm8Upp8&feature=PlayList&p=F59E8B6E4250AA8C&playnext=1&index=16

What about Gay Marriage? (parody)
http://www.youtube.com/watch?v=z5Ym7-AyQuQ

Leave it to Beaver retro special with Jane Pauley
http://www.youtube.com/watch?v=iFiHuPmV9-I

Father Knows Best clip (Thanksgiving) (1950s: traditional marriage and family TV drama)
http://www.youtube.com/watch?v=4Y1__b6uyxg

Father Knows Best clip (motor scooter)
http://www.youtube.com/watch?v=Jh2ZoMPBUwo

> See also opening and closing title segments for *Father Knows Best*:
> http://www.youtube.com/watch?v=U4AOmmoD7Lo (opening)
> http://www.youtube.com/watch?v=9GWkdrXCPyQ (closing

"Modern Woman: The Lost Sex" ('50s newsreel on the social evils of working wives)
http://www.youtube.com/watch?v=_2Rc63H7r6Y

Marital Advice: Secret for Men (comic skit)
http://www.youtube.com/watch?v=WJXUA1AwgYs

Marital Advice: Secret for Women (comic skit)
http://www.youtube.com/watch?v=6nVg0LtfKZU

Marriage: How to Have a Happy One (1950s public service ad, from a religious perspective)
http://www.youtube.com/watch?v=wjcNRpmp4tw

The Way Men Take Care of the Kids (comic skit)
http://www.youtube.com/watch?v=MsrmIaNJ_No

Chapter 10

To Sleep

Every night we all sleep, yet until recently, no one knew what actually happened during sleep. This chapter introduces students to some of the vast literature on sleep research and the problems that occur when we do not get enough sleep, a situation common to many students, especially those in late adolescence or early adulthood.

The chapter opens with "A Third of Life," an overview by Paul Martin, which describes the importance of sleep in the lives of humans and animals. Then Lawrence Epstein describes the physiology of sleep—what happens during sleep and the importance of different stages of sleep. Following this, the question of why adolescents particularly have problems getting enough sleep is explained in May A. Carskadon's "When Worlds Collide: Adolescent Need for Sleep Versus Societal Demands." William C. Dement and Christopher Vaughan, in "Sleep Debt and the Mortgaged Mind," argue that nothing about sleep is more important than understanding sleep deprivation and its cumulative effects on one's body and judgment. The opportunity to rate one's own sleep is next offered with "The Pittsburgh Sleep Quality Index," a self-scoring assessment devised by Daniel Buysse and others. The topic is then brought closer to home with "How Sleep Debt Hurts College Students," by June J. Pilcher and Amy S. Walters, as they explain the impact on the brain of pulling all-night study sessions. This is followed by Fred Danner and Barbara Phillips' study of the connection between sleep deprivation and teens' involvement in car crashes. The chapter concludes with "Poetry of Sleep," three poems on sleep by John Keats, Samuel Taylor Coleridge, and Lord Byron.

At the end of this chapter you will find video links to supplement the reading material about sleep disorders, the importance of sleep, and the need for adolescents to get enough sleep. In five parts, the "News Personality Stays Awake for 36 Hours" chronicles a reporter's 36 hours of sleep deprivation and the dangers of driving with little sleep.

A Third of Life (p. 466)

PAUL MARTIN

This reading, a selection from the first chapter of Martin's book, *Counting Sheep: The Science and Pleasures of Sleep and Dreams* (2002), provides a good background on sleep and introduces many terms, particularly "sleep debt," that students will encounter in the ensuing selections. Martin also describes the sleep habits of other creatures besides humans.

REVIEW QUESTIONS

1. Though sleep is a necessary behavior ("Nature imposes it upon us.") and we spend one-third of our lives doing it, sleep is strange in that, as a behavior, we do it alone. Most of the activity associated with sleep takes place in the brain and is invisible to observers; we have little recollection of it on waking; and scientifically speaking, we don't know definitively why we sleep.

2. Several signs of sleep deprivation: the near ubiquity of alarm clocks (which indicate that we are not waking when our bodies tell us we've had enough sleep); sleepiness and sleeping late on weekends and on holidays (which indicates a sleep debt the body is trying to pay back); and industrial and automobile accidents caused by sleepiness. Modern life leads to problems with sleepiness for several reasons: our sleep schedule is governed not by natural daylight but by electric lights; our culture places a high value on activity (constant motion), not rest; modern medicine doesn't offer much help because doctors receive virtually no training in sleep medicine.

3. The main characteristics of sleep: reduced sensory awareness; a "distinctive pattern of electrical activity in [the] brain;" a distinctive sleep posture that the organism generally maintains for an extended time in one place; a distinctive locale for sleep, generally secure and quiet; a predictable sleep/wake cycle. "According to these and other criteria, all mammals, birds, fish, amphibians, reptiles and insects that have been inspected have been found to sleep" (paragraph 27).

4. The brain is divided into hemispheres. For most species, both hemispheres enter deep sleep simultaneously. Dolphins—so that they can continue to surface for air, and many birds—so they can remain alert for predators—put one-half of their brains to sleep at a time. This unique way of sleeping is called unihemispheric sleep.

61

Improving Sleep, (p. 475)

LAWRENCE EPSTEIN, M.D., EDITOR

This reading, excerpted from a Harvard Special Health Report, clearly explains the widespread impact of sleep problems, how sleep changes over an individual's life, and the impact of various environmental factors on the quality of a person's sleep. Students may be particularly interested in how a lack of sleep impacts memory and learning, and the role on sleep quality of such common drugs as caffeine, alcohol, and nicotine.

REVIEW QUESTIONS

1. People with sleep problems put others at risk when operating machinery or making poor judgments in critical situations. Monetary costs associated with sleep disturbance are high: nearly $100 million for non-prescription sleeping aids; $50 million in caffeine tablets to fight sleepiness during the daytime; nearly $16 billion in medical treatment for sleep-related treatments.

2. For much of history, sleep was considered a passive state—defined as the absence of wakefulness. With the development of devices that could record brain activity however, researchers discovered that the brain is extremely active during sleep. Moreover, sleep is not a single state; it has stages, or an "architecture," with a recurring pattern. Non-REM (or quiet) sleep develops in four stages, each with a distinctive brain wave pattern, after a person has closed her eyes and reduced incoming stimulation. Stage 1 is light sleep, from which a person can readily be awakened. Stage 2, "the first stage of true sleep," lasts for one-half to three-quarters of an hour. The sleeper spends up to half the night in this stage. Sleepers spend about 20% of the night in stages 3 and 4, called "deep sleep" or "slow wave" sleep. Lasting for thirty-minute intervals, deep sleep plays a role in repairing the body and helps to refresh the sleeper on waking. During REM sleep, the body is essentially paralyzed but the brain is highly active, with rapid eye movements and raised temperature. Studies show that REM sleep "facilitates learning and memory." The sleeper enters REM sleep every 90 minutes or so, roughly 20% of the night.

3. Studies suggest that improvement in learning is lost if the sleeper does not get a full night's sleep. REM sleep is particularly important to learning. Interruptions to REM sleep decrease learning; interruptions to slow-wave sleep do not affect learning.

62

4. Sleep architecture refers to the "fairly predictable pattern" with which a sleeper cycles through stages of sleep during the night. The visual representation of a person's sleep architecture is called a hypnogram. A normal sleeper's sleep architecture consists of "four or five alternating non-REM and REM periods." Over a lifetime, a person's sleep architecture changes.

5. Circadian rhythm is a person's internal clock that regulates the ebb and flow of many of the body's patterns. The rhythm, or cycle, lasts roughly 24 hours and naturally inclines people to be sleepiest between 2 and 4 in the morning and between 2 and 3 in the afternoon. The body's circadian clock is located in a specific region of the hypothalamus and is sensitive to three influences: light, social/work schedules, and melatonin.

6. The stimulant caffeine affects sleep quality by remaining in the bloodstream, keeping people awake. It can increase the need to urinate. Nicotine, another stimulant, can affect sleepers with intense cravings that wake them at night. Alcohol interferes with REM sleep and causes sleepers to awake often, sometimes with nightmares. A sedentary lifestyle can lead to sleep problems, since sedentary people do not tax their muscles and therefore do not rest as completely as sleepers who are physically active. Exercise (though not too close to bedtime) promotes sleep, as can a regular schedule and a bedroom without cues that distract the sleeper from relaxing.

7. Sleep architecture changes through life. Infants sleep up to 18 hours a day. By age 6, that diminishes to 10 hours a night. Because of all of the changes occurring in their bodies, adolescents have greater sleep needs than pre-pubescent children but actually get less sleep per night and are often drowsy during the day. Through one's 20s, deep sleep decreases and wakings increase. The older the person, the more the nighttime wakings.

America's Sleep-Deprived Teens Nodding Off at School, Behind the Wheel (p. 487)

NATIONAL SLEEP FOUNDATION

This selection provides helpful data in the form of statistics that support the organization's claim that adolescent sleep debt is a national problem. Included in this reading is a boxed "Tips for Teens" (490), which sum up the National Sleep Foundation's recommendations.

REVIEW QUESTIONS

1. Only 20% of American teenagers get the "recommended nine hours of sleep on school nights, and nearly one-half (45%) sleep less than eight hours on school nights." Parents are largely clueless in their understanding of how much sleep their teenagers need, versus how much sleep they actually are getting. Ninety per cent of parents believe their children get enough sleep during the school week, but only one-half (56%) of students feel they do. Nearly a third of adolescents who believe they have a sleep problem have not reported this to a parent.

2. Teenagers typically miss twelve hours of sleep each week. Insufficient sleep in this "critical period of development and growth" can lead to compromised performance in school, dangerously drowsy driving, emotional strain, and sedentary lifestyle.

3. Adolescence is a "critical period of development—academically, emotionally and physically," according to sleep experts. Teenagers without sufficient sleep are like people without sufficient nutrients, operating at a significant deficit. Sleep is needed to restore the body and to process daily learning.

4. A "phase delay" is a shifting of the circadian, or internal, clock of teenagers, making them more wakeful at night and prompting them to sleep later each morning. When a phase-delayed adolescent faces an early school start time (and, hence, an early wake time), significant sleep debt can result.

5. The NSF survey reports that 31% of teenagers take naps. Sleepy adolescents try *making up for* missed sleep by napping instead of napping *to complement* normal sleep. Napping is not sufficient for reducing sleep debt. Experts recommend that daytime naps be limited to forty-five minutes in order not to interfere with nighttime sleep.

6. "Rollercoaster" sleep, according to sleep expert Mary Carskadon, is "irregular sleep" that occurs when teenagers try to catch up on missed weekday sleep by napping and sleeping late on weekends. Irregular sleep patterns negatively affect performance and mood.

7. Consumer electronics, such as video games, televisions, computers, and phones in the bedroom, stimulate teenagers, which make getting to sleep more difficult. The survey reports that adolescents "with four or more such items in their bedrooms are much more likely than their peers to get an insufficient amount of sleep at night and almost twice as likely to fall asleep in school and while doing homework."

When Worlds Collide: Adolescent Need for Sleep Versus Societal Demands (p. 493)

MARY CARSKADON

Sleep expert Mary Carskadon has written widely on the topic of adolescent sleep. Here, in a chapter from her book *Adolescent Sleep Needs and School Starting Times* (1999), she reviews the various reasons why adolescents do not get the sleep they need—and makes a case for adjusting school scheduling.

REVIEW QUESTIONS

1. Adolescents shift their hours of wakefulness and sleep: they go to sleep later and wake later than do pre-adolescents. There is evidence that biological changes in adolescence contribute to this phase delay in the circadian rhythm. Phase delay conflicts directly with fixed school start times. For reasons they cannot control behaviorally, adolescents' body clocks make them sleepiest at exactly the time the social world (i.e., school) demands that they be most alert.

2. Sleep researchers discovered that adolescents, "regardless of age or developmental stage," needed *more*, not less, sleep than younger children: roughly 9.25 hours per night. Older adolescents also had later waking times (8 AM) than younger adolescents, confirming the reported shifting of adolescent sleep schedules. This delay in sleep patterns has been observed among adolescents in North and South America, Asia, Australia, and Europe. A final result: older adolescents tended to be sleepier than younger adolescents, even though they slept the same amount of time the evening before.

3. Several behavioral and social factors influence adolescent sleep. Parents stop setting bed times as their children age. Older children have more academic demands placed on them and have more social opportunities outside the home. Many adolescents also work, sometimes as much as 20 hours each

week. Consumer electronics in bedrooms can interfere with sleep. Finally, fixed starting times for school affect adolescent sleep. Based on ease of scheduling buses and after-school activities, school districts tend to schedule younger children for later start times and adolescents for earlier start times—exactly reversing the naturally occurring sleep patterns of children.

4. "Process S" ("sleep/wake homeostasis") is the model that describes a countervailing balance between the impulse to sleep and the impulse to stay awake. The longer one is awake, the greater the impulse to sleep; the "closer one is to having slept, the less pressure there is to sleep." The ebb and flow of wakefulness and sleepiness in sleep/wake homeostasis can be measured in two ways: through the MSLT, which tests sleepiness—the speed with which someone falls asleep—and the EEG, which measures brain wave activity suggestive of deep sleep. "Process C" ("circadian timing system") describes the complex workings of the body's internal clock, which is aligned with the 24-hour clock and light/dark cues. Researchers can mark the high and low points (the times of greatest alertness and greatest sleepiness) by measuring the secretion of the hormone melatonin.

5. The colliding worlds of Carskadon's title are the scheduling demands of school and work coming into conflict with the changes in adolescent behavior and circadian biology (see Review Questions 1 and 3). These changes can shift adolescent schedules of wakefulness/sleepiness from morning preference to evening preference. An adolescent's internal clock can then go "out of phase" with the external clock (i.e., the scheduling expectations) of the adult, social world. Severe sleepiness and sleep debt can result, leading to "marked impairment"—degraded performance in school and emotional turmoil.

Sleep Debt and the Mortgaged Mind (p. 501)

WILLIAM C. DEMENT AND CHRISTOPHER VAUGHAN

Another founding pioneer in the study of sleep, William C. Dement, along with co-author Christopher Vaughan, considers how lack of sleep can accumulate into a sleep "debt," a medical condition that has played a role in such recent tragedies as the oil spill from the *Exxon Valdez* and the *Challenger* space shuttle explosion. By this point in the readings, students might be motivated to consider their own sleep habits.

1. In the popular press, the cause of the *Exxon Valdez* oil spill was the captain's drunkenness. The National Transportation Safety Board actually concluded that the "direct cause . . . was the behavior of the third mate, who had slept only 6 hours in the previous 48 and was severely sleep deprived."

2. Dement warns that drowsiness is not an early warning sign but the last stage before nodding off to sleep. With the onset of head-nodding drowsiness, a person can drop off to sleep "instantly." People should be alert to the danger sign and should seek rest immediately—and, in particular, should stop operating machinery.

3. The "continuum of sleepiness and alertness" is the relative measure of a person's wakefulness. Where a person is on this scale at any given moment determines level of performance.

4. The drive to sleep is like the primary drive to eat or drink. When the body is deprived of food, it gets hungry. Deprived of water, a person gets thirsty. Deprived of sleep, a person gets sleepy. The brain keeps an exact tally of sleep debt. The more sleep deprived a person is, the more the brain will work to make the person drowsy and get sleep—to pay back the "debt." In the same way, the brain impels a hungry person to eat and a thirsty person to drink.

5. Sleep debt is the accumulated amount of sleep lost over a period of days or longer. Sleep debt is "additive." Lack of sleep one night adds onto the sleep debt accumulated on successive nights, so that a person who loses two hours of sleep on three successive nights accumulates a six-hour cumulative debt. The results: impaired "energy, mood, and cognition." We must assume that "[u]ntil proven otherwise," a sleep debt must be repaid, "perhaps even hour for hour." The "size of the sleep debt and its dangerous effects are definitely directly related to the amount of lost sleep."

6. If a person has accumulated a severe sleep debt over several days or weeks, getting a full night's sleep, or even extra sleep on a given night, will be restorative but not completely so. Following the principle that every hour of debt must be repaid, one night of ten-hour sleep repays two hours (the "full" eight plus an extra two). If the debt is larger than the repaid number of hours, the person will continue to feel sleepy.

67

7. A study at the Henry Ford Hospital Sleep Disorders Center clearly showed that alcohol greatly increases the sleepiness of a person who has accumulated a sleep debt. People at a party may not get a full night's rest. Drinking on top of sleep debt exacerbates sleepiness and is thus a "co-conspirator" in many alcohol-related accidents. A "large sleep debt and even a small amount of alcohol can create a fatal 'fatigue.'"

The Pittsburgh Sleep Quality Index (p. 510)

DANIEL BUYSSE

After reading a chapter's worth of materials on the negative effects of sleep deprivation and given our natural fascination with taking self-assessments, students should be curious to know how they fare on a standardized measure of sleep quality. You might ask students to take the assessment before they read any of the articles on sleep, to elicit a fresh response untouched by their knowledge of the field. Conversely, you might decide that first sensitizing students to sleep-related issues will prompt in them a more thoughtful self-assessment. Students will want to score the assessment and, given human nature, compare scores. You may or may not want to encourage this sharing, deeming it personal or sensitive data. In an effort to generate some perspective on the assessment, you might recommend that students complete one or two of the accompanying Discussion and Writing Suggestions.

There are no review questions for this selection.

How Sleep Debt Hurts College Students (p. 516)

JUNE J. PILCHER AND AMY S. WALTERS

This selection is one of two in the chapter that presents findings of a scientific study. Students may have difficulty with the concepts and language of statistics which figure prominently in the Results section. But a background in statistics is not necessary to appreciate the experimenters' results: that college students can sabotage their own success by staying up all night studying. The selection will likely spark interest among those who have pulled all-nighters, perhaps a majority of the class. One likely point of discussion will be how students reading this piece will use (or not use) the authors' conclusions in modifying their own behavior.

There are no review questions for this selection.

Adolescent Sleep, School Start Times, and Teen Motor Vehicle Crashes (p.526)

FRED DANNER AND BARBARA PHILLIPS

Fred Danner and Barbara Phillips present evidence that shows a correlation between adolescents' lack of sufficient sleep and the incidence of car crashes. Danner and Phillips point out that adding just one hour of sleep per day during the week has a significant impact on driving safety.

There are no review questions for this selection.

Poetry of Sleep (p. 533)

JOHN KEATS, LORD BYRON, SAMUEL TAYLOR COLERIDGE

Three poets from the English Romantic period give us three personal views of sleep. John Keats begs for sleep, the "embalmer of the still midnight"; Samuel Taylor Coleridge recounts the terrors inherent in nightmares, "the fiendish dream"; and Lord Byron reveals the power of dreaming: "dreams in their development have breath,/ And tears, and tortures, and the touch of joy."

There are no review questions for the poems.

VIDEO LINKS

Falling Asleep While Driving ("Carcam" video of accident)
   http://www.youtube.com/watch?v=DxLdCC46BUs&feature=related

News Personality Stays Awake for 36 Hours
   Part I
   http://www.youtube.com/watch?v=1K1ylwgYLIE

   Part II
   http://www.youtube.com/watch?v=FT1taRi19n0

   Part III
   http://www.youtube.com/watch?v=-QLfwDpnZwo&feature=related

Part IV
http://www.youtube.com/watch?v=_2zVNufE5yg&feature=related

Part V
http://www.youtube.com/watch?v=G4ncaKNR_Ko&feature=related

Your Night in a Sleep Lab
http://www.youtube.com/watch?v=pzGwaFnamKQ&feature=related

Sleep Disorders
Sleep Disorders overview
http://www.youtube.com/watch?v=X2yfUL8uct0&feature=related

What do sleep disorders do?
http://www.youtube.com/watch?v=evvYmnIhG78&feature=related

Ads to Promote Better Teen Sleeping
College Sleep Commercial
http://www.youtube.com/watch?v=68ERFt8rN8E&feature=related
The Importance of Sleep for Headbanging/Moshing (comic animation)
http://www.youtube.com/watch?v=8eKbyCqVUD8

Chapter 11

New and Improved: Six Decades of Advertising

The readings in this section consider that, even though advertising methods and styles have changed from the post-WWII era, the psychological techniques that worked in earlier advertising have remained the same. The chapter therefore invites students to speculate on certain qualities of human nature that may remain constant over time (over the last 60 years, at least) and the ways in which we remain susceptible to certain appeals. While students interested in journalism and merchandising will gravitate to this chapter, all students will find in the subject of advertising an excellent opportunity to practice the techniques of analysis introduced in Chapter 6. You may want your students to bring other advertisements to class for discussion in addition to those provided in the chapter. And you may want to use the selections in this chapter to discuss the principles of visual rhetoric and design.

The reading selections provide students with the language for classifying different psychological appeals. In "Advertising's Fifteen Basic Appeals," Jib Fowles lists the psychological needs that advertisers target through graphics and in texts. More technical vocabulary is introduced in Courtland L. Bovée, John V. Thille, George P. Dovel, and Marian Burk Wood's "Making the Pitch in Print Advertising," which explains how an ad's textual components work together. Then Behrens and Rosen direct students to view two segments of the hit television show *Mad Men* about the advertising business. The critical nuclei of the chapter follow: "A Portfolio of Print Advertisements" and a "Portfolio of TV Commercials." The print ad portfolio offers a selection of 28 full-page advertisements for cigarettes, alcoholic beverages, automobiles, and other products, that appeared in American and British magazines over the past sixty years. The television ad portfolio which stretches from the 1960s to the 2000s covers some of the same products but also—because of the opportunities afforded by video—some strikingly different approaches to advertising. Students should be invited to use the analytical tools in the earlier part of the chapter to discuss and extract meaning from the ads, either singly or in combination.

In addition to the commercials in the "Portfolio of TV Commercials," the authors offer additional TV commercials in video links provided at the end of this

71

chapter. David Ogilvy, at times referred to as the Father of Advertising, discusses advertising in the first link listed.

Advertising's Fifteen Basic Appeals (p. 539)

JIB FOWLES

In "Advertising's Fifteen Basic Appeals," an article from *Advertising and Popular Culture*, Jib Fowles draws upon Henry A. Murray's research to produce a psychological analysis of advertising. Following the discussion of analysis in Chapter 6, students can evaluate Fowles' classification of the fifteen basic appeals of advertising, noting that it is based on the assumption that advertisers frequently attempt to bypass logical reasoning to appeal to consumers' emotional needs. Additionally, this article can serve as a principle source and guide for students' analysis of current advertisements. Students will need to focus on the emotional appeals of an ad rather than the product itself—something that takes a bit of practice. It is also important for students to examine where the advertisement is placed, whether in a certain type of magazine or newspaper, on a billboard or the Internet, or on television. Note that Fowles points out that any given ad may rely upon more than a single appeal, though there is generally one primary appeal.

REVIEW QUESTIONS

1. In the United States the supply of consumer goods greatly exceeds demand, so manufacturers attempt to create and increase demand through advertising. Where goods are scarcer and demand is high, there is less need for advertising to persuade consumers to select and purchase particular products.

2. Advertisers often divide the (customer's) mind into two halves. The bottom half (the most primal) consists of "unfulfilled urges and motives," such as "[l]usts, ambitions, tendernesses, vulnerabilities," which cannot be given full expression in the real world. (These sometimes unconscious drives and feelings correspond to what Freud described as the id.) The upper half of the mind consists of those rational and acceptable behaviors that allow people to function in society and which serve as a kind of façade for the more primitive impulses bubbling below. (The upper half of the mind corresponds to what Freud described as the ego and the superego.) It is the advertiser's job to penetrate the façade of the upper half of the mind and appeal to those more powerful but often unarticulated and less socially acceptable drives that

72

reside in the bottom half. The way in, "the softest points of entrée," are those appeals that Fowles describes in the remainder of his article.

3. Most advertisements, according to Fowles, appeal to (1) "deep running drives" in consumers' minds; i.e., the emotional or "elemental" appeal and (2) information about the product; i.e., the rational or logical appeal.

4. Fowles' fifteen basic appeals of advertising are essentially a refinement of a "full taxonomy of needs" originally developed by Henry Murray, a psychologist at the Harvard Psychological Clinic, and described in his book *Explorations in Personality*. Based on his analysis of numerous advertisements, Murray classified the appeals into twenty human motives. Fowles, with help from his students, reduced these to eighteen and then to fifteen.

5. Ads employing appeals to sex and to the need to aggress carry significant risk of backfire, according to Fowles. Consumers may be offended by such ads; overt sexual content may strike some as verging on the pornographic, and the destructive impulses in ads employing aggressive appeals may become associated with the product itself.

6. The use of humor or of celebrities or of the past or future are not considered separate appeals by Fowles; rather they are considered "styles" in furtherance of making one or more of the fifteen appeals. Thus, humor is sometimes used to temper an appeal to aggress or a negative appeal to affiliation; celebrities are used in support of an appeal to the need for guidance or to the need for attention.

Making the Pitch in Print Advertising (p. 558)

COURTLAND BOVÉE, JOHN V. THILLE, GEORGE P. DOVEL, and MARIAN BURK WOOD

Along with the previous article by Fowles, this selection will help students analyze the print advertisements they encounter. The selection directs readers to consider the function of headlines and body text in typical ads. Encourage students to bring ads to class (specify *photocopies* of ads they find in the library!) that illustrate some of the principles discussed in this selection.

73

1. Copywriting can be an art, but it is primarily a business enterprise: though successful copywriters must love language and use their imaginations and stylistic skills, their main purpose is to sell the product.

2. Main types of headlines: news headlines, emotional headlines, benefit headlines, directive headlines, offbeat and curiosity headlines, hornblowing headlines.

3. Main types of body copy styles: straight-line copy, narrative copy, dialogue/monolog copy, picture-and-caption copy.

Selling Happiness: Two Pitches from Mad Men *(p. 563)*

These two video clips from the award-winning TV show *Mad Men* give students an "inside" view of the advertising business, the "unique selling proposition" (USP) designed to make consumers eager to buy the client's product. Both videos show how the advertiser manipulates language—even truth—to create a selling edge for the client's product.

There are no review questions for these videos.

A Portfolio of Print Advertisements *(p. 564)*

In this collection of 28 advertisements, the authors offer a sampling of different print advertising techniques. Some of these images will be familiar to students; others may strike them as being very sexist. Following Fowles's perspective, students may consider the type of emotional appeals used in individual advertisements and ask if the appeal addresses the need for sex, the need for group approval, the need to escape, the need for security or other types of appeals. You may wish to make overheads of the advertisements in order to point out how the viewer's eye is moved through what is pictured, such as the gaze of the models or the viewing angle and the balance between different elements.

Students can be alerted to the use of problem/solution narrative structure, the relative positioning of men and women in the advertisements, the dress and general appearance of the models, the use of cultural icons, and the use of slogans to direct attention and increase brand recall. In addition to using the analytical tools introduced earlier in the chapter, students can also look at advertisements just to see how particular products are sold, as examples of how appeals change from one time to another, or as displays of cultural characteristics of their time (e.g., marriage roles, the sexual appeal of alcohol and smoking). Students can be encouraged to seek out additional advertisements from the library and *photocopy them*. Back issues of *Life* or *Time* magazines will be especially good for this.

You may wish to direct students' attention to keynote events that triggered social change and discuss how events such as World War II, the post-war search for normalcy, the development of the suburbs, the baby boom, and the civil rights and women's movements are reflected in these advertisements. Especially in the alcohol advertisements, students will observe appeals to sex aimed at the male consumer. The Ballantine Ale ad from the 1950s, for example, depicts more women than men, all of them having an obviously good time. And in the Bacardi Rum advertisement of the 1960s, we see three women grouped around a single man. The two on the left direct their gaze to the pouring liquid, while the third woman on the right looks to the viewer. The scenario suggests a popular spy film of the era, a reference strengthened in the text's reference to "our man Fernando."

There are no review questions for this section.

A Portfolio of TV Commercials (p. 601)

This collection of television commercials from the 1960s to the 2000s offers a wide range of examples of the different techniques employed in TV ads. Many of the ads, like the *Energizer: Darth Vader* and the *Sony Bravia: Bunnies* commercials, rely on viewers' cultural savvy for their impact. Others present clever visual analogues to their verbal message (*Honda: Physics*; *Jeep: Snow Covered*) or employ humor (*Alka Seltzer: Spicy Meatball*; *Tide to Go: Interview*) or sex appeal (*Chanel No. 5: Share the Fantasy*; *Levi's: Launderette*). At least one of the commercials is puzzling (*The Gap: Pardon Our Dust*) and was pulled off the air shortly after it was released. Some, like the *Union Carbide: Chick* commercial captivate the viewer by the voiceover's reinforcement of the visual message. Each commercial affords students the opportunity for summarizing and for applying the principles discussed by Fowles.

There are no review questions for the section.

A Conversation about Advertising with David Ogilvy (celebrated ad man)
http://www.youtube.com/watch?v=0kfsnjcUNiw&feature=PlayList&p=A34797FA8F45C78F&playnext=1&index=1

How to Get Ahead in Advertising (1989)
http://www.youtube.com/watch?v=VWPzRxPdlkU&feature=PlayList&p=A34797FA8F45C78F&playnext=1&index=2

Advertising: What Psychological Tricks Do They Use?
http://www.youtube.com/watch?v=XtvHNfomZL8&feature=PlayList&p=A34797FA8F45C78F&index=0&playnext=1

How to be Creative in Advertising
http://www.youtube.com/watch?v=QvJoc8oEays

Old Man Men (Retired ad executive Bill Blackshaw)
http://www.youtube.com/watch?v=zwLhcFwvoeE

Additional TV Commercials

Note: Unless otherwise indicated, all commercials listed were produced in U.S.A

American Tourister Luggage: Gorilla (Doyle, Dane, Bernbach,1969)
http://www.youtube.com/watch?v=B2ZeIoLz8FE

Campbells Soup: Winter Commercial*
http://www.youtube.com/watch?v=4PdeGx1obvc

Chevrolet: "Baseball, Hot Dogs, Apple Pie" (Campbell-Ewald, 1969)*
http://www.youtube.com/watch?v=_rYXmWY9HY4

Coca Cola: "Hilltop" ("I'd Like to Buy the World a Coke") (McCann-Erickson Worldwide, 1971)
http://www.youtube.com/watch?v=FvTqW6on8MA

Dunlop: "Tested for the Unexpected" (Abbott Mead Vickers, BBDO, UK, 1993)
http://www.youtube.com/watch?v=NLWWtgqDG2M

Hovis: "Bike Ride" (Collett Dickenson Pearce, UK, 1973)* [shot by Ridley Scott]
http://www.youtube.com/watch?v=CFLBvLxLJMI

Apple: Macintosh (Chiat/Day, 1984)
http://www.youtube.com/watch?v=OYecfV3ubP8

The Guardian: "Points of View" (Boase Massimi Pollitt, UK, 1987)
http://www.youtube.com/watch?v=E3h-T3KQNxU

Lego: "Kipper" (TWBA, UK, 1980)
http://www.youtube.com/watch?v=V2nL5sSSvd0

Basf: "Dear John" (Whitaker Advertising, New Zealand, 1979)
http://www.youtube.com/watch?v=CD6S8DZHpG4

Volkswagen: "Changes" (BMP/DBD Needham, UK, 1988)
http://www.youtube.com/watch?v=DMtdPXPejZ0

Energizer: "Bunny Introduction" (TBWA Chiat/Day, 1989)
http://www.youtube.com/watch?v=fILdYrxnrf8

Swedish Televerket: "Noxin" (HLR Drumfabriken/BBDO, Sweden, 1993)
http://www.youtube.com/watch?v=0LhuyMjxNfA

Xerox: "Monks" (Needham Harper Steers, 1975)
http://www.youtube.com/watch?v=EPPOgl-9GVM

Little Caesar's Pizza: "Training Camp" (Cliff Freeman and Partners, 1994)
http://www.youtube.com/watch?v=HBdi0q6TXbw

Sony Trinitron: "Lifespan" (Boase Massimi Pollitt, UK, 1984)
http://www.youtube.com/watch?v=UlU6crWC_3Q

Hebrew National: "Higher Authority" (1975)
http://www.youtube.com/watch?v=Qf2j-YzZRAA

American Express: "Stephen King: (Ogilvy & Mather, 1984)
http://www.youtube.com/watch?v=fLB8Rx6FzOE

California Milk Processor Board: "Got Milk? Heaven"
(Goodby Silverstein & Partners, 1996)
http://www.youtube.com/watch?v=Dh6098zpxWY

Democratic National Committee: "Daisy Girl" (Doyle, Dane
Bernbach, 1964)
http://www.youtube.com/watch?v=OKs-bTL-
pRg&feature=PlayList&p=B81F617C1157
DFDD&playnext=1&index=53

Keep America Beautiful: "Crying Indian" (Marsteller, Inc., 1970)
http://www.youtube.com/watch?v=j7OHG7tHrNM

Ameriquest Mortgage: "Plane Ride"
http://www.youtube.com/watch?v=LIjY_-5BK6k

Chapter 12

Fairy Tales: A Closer Look at Cinderella

Many feel that fairy tale literature should be off limits to aggressive, critical inquiry. "A Closer Look at 'Cinderella'" presents students with the opportunity to challenge this view. The readings here raise several questions: to what extent does critical inquiry illuminate? obscure? make something of nothing? In attempting to answer these questions, students will themselves invoke critical distinctions—perhaps similar to those we've included here; "Cinderella" may be approached as literature (Thompson) or as an occasion for psychological inquiry (Bettelheim). By first reading the nine variants of "Cinderella," students will be able to make their own critical observations of the tale and then compare these with the observations made by professionals.

This chapter begins with a reminiscence by Arthur Schlesinger, Jr., about his mother's reading to him when he was a child and the world of imagination that it opened to him. Next, Stith Thompson provides a general introduction to fairy tale literature. The variants of "Cinderella" follow, the modern variants (which can be read as a subunit) being those by Disney and Anne Sexton. The chapter ends with appraisals of the tale by Cullen, Bettelheim, Panttaja, Rossner, Poniewozik, and Orenstein.

The variants of the story lend themselves quite naturally to comparison and contrast. Opportunities for critique and argument abound and the selection by Bettelheim is complex enough to make summaries worthwhile.

Variations of the story of Cinderella have not only been the subject of movies, but also of opera and ballet. To see some excerpts of these adaptations, go to the video links that appear at the end of this chapter.

What Great Books Do for Children (p. 617)

ARTHUR SCHLESINGER, JR.

Arthur Schlesinger, Jr.'s imagination was expanded by the fairy tales and stories his mother first read to him and which he later read to himself. Through them, he vicariously experienced the terrors, human flaws, conflicts, and "voyages of discovery" that all good literature engenders.

There are no review questions for this selection.

Universality of the Folktale (p. 619)

STITH THOMPSON

This selection introduces the idea that folk tales are worthy of serious reading and analysis. Stith Thompson concentrates here on the definition and history of the folktale thus offering an excellent overview of the chapter in addition to providing material for student analysis papers. Students should read this selection directly before or after the variants of "Cinderella" and certainly before any of the critical examinations (namely, those by Bettelheim and Panttaja). The final paragraph, and especially the final sentence, of Thompson's selection may be of special interest in establishing a mood of acceptance, or at least tolerance, of the various analyses of "Cinderella."

REVIEW QUESTIONS

1. The storyteller is treasured by societies for providing information and amusement; inspiration (both secular and religious), and stimulation, as well as escape from routine.

2. Thompson claims that the most significant difference between the folktale and modern fiction is the traditional nature of folk material—tales that are not original in our sense of the word but that are passed along skillfully, bearing the authority of great age and constituting an act of conservation and reverence. Moreover, a folktale is meant to be listened to, not read.

3. Religion involves an attempt to understand personal, tribal, and cosmic origins; folktales are concerned generally with the "olden days." Their own origins are prehistoric, as are religion's.

4. The same tale is often dispersed widely throughout different parts of the world.

Seven Variants of "Cinderella" (p. 623)

The Perrault and Grimm versions of "Cinderella" are placed first (not in chronological order), since these will be the most familiar to students, and the Anne Sexton poem is placed last, a poet's rendering of the tale. Five of the variants of the tale—Perrault, Grimm, Tuan Ch'êng-shih, and the African and Native American versions—can be compared and contrasted to the so-called "traditional" renderings of "Cinderella." The explicitly modern versions by Disney and Sexton might be compared as a subset. Comparisons and contrasts can obviously be drawn between the traditional and modern versions, with students arguing the various interests and strengths of each. This chapter presents students with an excellent opportunity to practice their own analysis of primary material before reading the analyses of scholars and writers.

The Rise of Perrault's "Cinderella" (p. 645)

BONNIE CULLEN

This selection provides extremely helpful background on the most familiar of the Cinderella tales as Bonnie Cullen answers the question of how is it, among all the versions of the tale available, that we came to accept Charles Perrault's version as the standard. Her discussion points out thematic commonalities among the versions while also noting that Perrault's version most strongly reinforces conventional views of femininity.

REVIEW QUESTIONS

1. The classic thematic elements, shared by all versions of the tale: "an abused child, rescue through some incarnation of the dead mother, recognition, and marriage." (See ¶1.)

2. Folk tales were of the "peasant class" (¶11) and were less concerned with manners and morals than with the resourcefulness of its characters and with action (sometimes brutal—Zezolla kills her stepmother). Fairy tale versions of folk tales like "Cinderella" were "a new literary genre" written with an eye to court life in seventeenth-century France. The tales were offered "as a kind of conversational game" for salons. As such, in the case of Perrault's "Cinderella," they became tales about manners, wit, and irony, modeling courtly virtues that gentlemen would find appealing in a wife.

3. The Romantic movement in the nineteenth century prompted the Grimm brothers to look to the "country folk," closer to nature, for "some primal wisdom" lacking in Perrault's mannered tale.

4. Of the three Cinderellas, Perrault's is the least active and is "the best vehicle for Victorian notions of femininity." (See ¶21.) The Cinderella of both D'Aulnoy and the Grimms are more resourceful and take more direct control of their own fates than does Perrault's character. Also, Perrault's "Cinderella" shifts power away from Cinderella and to the fairy godmother.

5. Perrault's version of "Cinderella" became canonical, the "standard" version, in the nineteenth century. At the time, the market for fairy tales was the English middle class, whose interests inclined them to stories about urban life and "the social sphere, rather than the forest" of the Grimm brothers. The key paragraph in Cullen that explains Perrault's emergence is ¶20: D'Aulnoy's Cinderella "is busy slaying ogres and galloping through the mud;" Aschenputtel's sisters are hacking up their feet and getting their eyes pecked out. In nineteenth-century England, parents selecting the tales were looking to "improve" the minds of young people and make them fit for society. Perrault's "Cinderella," a model of Victorian propriety, emerged as the standard.

"Cinderella": A Story of Sibling Rivalry and Oedipal Conflicts (p. 651)
BRUNO BETTELHEIM

Bettelheim's analysis of "Cinderella," excerpted from *The Uses of Enchantment,* is one of the longer and more complex selections in the text. The author's psychoanalytic premise is summarized in Discussion Question 1 (p. 658), and students may profit by reading this question as they prepare for class discussion or their own summaries. The principal assumption—that complex unconscious and subconscious mechanisms explain human behavior—may prove difficult for some students, especially as it is applied to the apparently innocent "Cinderella." Bettelheim's intricate analysis can demonstrate how arguments follow from their premises and how, if students want to object, they should examine the argument's premises and the consistency of their application. After becoming familiar with Bettelheim's approach, students may be interested in viewing Stephen Sondheim's musical *Into the Woods* (1988), a fusion of fairy tales that was inspired by Bettelheim's writing.

REVIEW QUESTIONS

1. Living among the ashes symbolizes sibling rivalry and Cinderella's debased condition.

2. The stepsisters in "Cinderella" may be a device "to explain and make acceptable an animosity which one wishes would not exist among true siblings."

3. A child experiencing sibling rivalry may feel that a parent is overlooking his or her welfare for the welfare of another child; the child may also feel persecuted at the hands of a sibling and believe that the parent is indifferent to this persecution.

4. Through Cinderella's triumph, the child gains "exaggerated hopes for his future which he needs to counteract the extreme misery" of sibling rivalry.

5. The fantasy solution to "Cinderella" is appropriate for children in that children do not believe they can actually reverse their fortunes; children also gain relief through fantasies of glory and domination over their siblings.

6. The child who identifies with Cinderella reasons that since Cinderella's goodness is eventually acknowledged by all, so too, one day, will his or her goodness be acknowledged.

7. By comparison with the vileness of the stepmother and stepsisters, the child feels his inadequacies and wrongdoings are minor. The vileness of these characters also justifies whatever harm is done to them in the story.

8. Cinderella's paradox is that she believes herself to be superior to her stepmother and stepsisters but at the same time feels that she deserves her degraded state.

Cinderella: **Not** *So Morally Superior (p. 658)*

ELISABETH PANTTAJA

Students should compare the Grimm version with the Disney version before reading this article in order to understand, in the former version, the influence of Cinderella's mother's magic in helping Cinderella. In her analysis of the tale, Elisabeth Panttaja argues that, contrary to more common understanding of

83

Cinderella as beautiful and morally superior, she is neither. Nor is she, for practical purposes, "motherless." And, Panttaja concludes, Cinderella and the prince did not marry for love. Panttaja's reading of the tale is revisionist; that is, her reading forces us to revise our own thinking about and interpretation of the tale.

Panttaja is working from a slightly longer 1857 version of "Cinderella," and students may find some inconsistencies with the story as reprinted in their textbook. The longer version of the tale can be found in Jack Zipes' *The Great Fairy Tale Tradition* (Norton, 2001).

REVIEW QUESTIONS

1. The opening scene of the fairy tale sets out the problem to be overcome in the story. In "Cinderella," this problem is the heroine's lack of a mother. When she can overcome this, she will succeed.

2. Despite the fact that she dies at the beginning of the story, Cinderella's mother remains an active, positive presence in the story for Cinderella. She is present in the magical hazel tree, present in the form of birds who come to help her sort the lentils, present in the doves/pigeons who poke out the eyes of the stepsisters and tell the prince to look for blood in the shoe, and present in the protection Cinderella finds in the dovecote/pear tree. Panttaja states that not only is Cinderella not alone, her mother's magical powers are what help her triumph (that is, marry the prince) at the end of the story.

3. Through her magical interventions, Cinderella's mother directly blunts the designs of the stepmother and wins for Cinderella the prince's hand in marriage. The mother, then, is wily (helping with the plans to win the prince), determined, and apparently ruthless, inasmuch as the pigeons/doves that aid Cinderella with the lentils peck out the eyes of her stepsisters as a punishment. As Panttaja says: "She does for Cinderella exactly what the wicked stepmother wishes to do for her own daughters."

4. Panttaja's thesis is that Cinderella and her mother are not morally superior to the stepsisters and their mother. As a practical matter, Cinderella (who is usually understood as patient and long suffering) must scheme to get her way. In wining the hand of the prince, her "virtue" plays no part. What wins the prince is Cinderella's willingness to perform "subversive acts: she

disobeys the stepmother, enlists forbidden helpers, uses magic powers, lies, hides, dissembles, disguises herself, and evades pursuit."

5. Romantic love plays no significant role in Cinderella's eventual union with the prince. Panttaja points out that nowhere do these characters profess love for each other. The prince is literally charmed by the magical spell of Cinderella's dress. He is enchanted by the mother, not by Cinderella's "piety, which he has never experienced, nor by her own beauty." The prince is won through the mother's "power and manipulation," not through any "romance or affection" between him and Cinderella.

6. Disguises and enchantments in fairy tale literature often appear in stories that feature an unusual marriage—say, between a mortal and a deity or between an ordinary person and someone of nobility. The disguise, which temporarily blinds or confuses, enables a person to "enter into a marriage that he or she would not normally enter into, usually one that crosses class lines."

I Am Cinderella's Stepmother and I Know My Rights (p. 662)

JUDITH ROSSNER

Novelist Judith Rossner considers the story of Cinderella from the stepmother's viewpoint—what if she were to sue for defamation of character? The humorous complaint of the stepmother nicely establishes her viewpoint but it also provides ideas for a comparison of the Disney and Grimm versions.

There are no review questions for this reading.

The Princess Paradox (p. 666)

JAMES PONIEWOZIK

In discussing movies based on the Cinderella story, James Poniewozik points out that the impact that feminism has had on depictions of Cinderella-based characters, for instance that the new "Cinderella" is likely to save her prince—rather than the other way around—and while she still must be pretty, she must also be smart and independent.

REVIEW QUESTIONS

1. In the new Cinderella movies, the prince is an unimportant character who must adjust to his fate (becoming king), maturing into the role. The princess,

85

by contrast, must actively make her fate. She must be smart, feisty, and skeptical of her role as princess. Girls are the active principle in these movies; boys, the passive.

2. Poniewozik suggests that the makers of the new Cinderella movies want to "have-your-tiara-and-disdain-it-too." That is, they depict heroines who unashamedly embrace the role of princess; at the same time, to ensure a feminist appeal, the filmmakers create Cinderellas who are strong, ambitious, and career focused in ways that disparage the traditional princess role. These modern Cinderellas have the best of both worlds; they get to enjoy the prerogatives of being a princess only after they have re-invented the role by asserting their independence.

3. Movies like *Charlie's Angels* and *Crouching Tiger, Hidden Dragon* showed heroines who were as resourceful, strong, and physically dangerous as their male counterparts. The new wave of Cinderella movies shows women who are equally talented and resourceful but who permit themselves, as well, to embrace the role of Cinderella—as long as they get to re-define that role in ways that do not require submission to male authority.

4. On this point Poniewozik writes as follows: "the new Cinderella has developed rules and conventions as strict as a Joseph Campbell template. She should be pretty, but in a class-president way, not a head-cheerleader way. She should be able to stand up for herself (recall the *Crouching Tiger* moves of *Shrek*'s Princess Fiona). She must be socially conscious—a result, says Meg Cabot, author of the *Princess Diaries* books, of Princess Diana's charitable work. And she should above all not want to be a princess—at least until she changes her mind."

Cinderella and Princess Culture (p. 670)

PEGGY ORENSTEIN

Peggy Orenstein discusses the multi-billion dollar business of Disney's Princess Culture—the marketing of anything (phones, clothing, bedding) that allows a girl to tap into the princess fantasy. Orenstein worries about the long-term impact of the Princess Culture on little girls' self-esteem.

1. The Princess line is Disney's successful effort at packaging its princesses into a single commercial enterprise independent of the animated features in which the separate princesses originally appeared. Thus, Cinderella, Snow White, and other princesses are featured in the ads "under one royal rubric," capitalizing on what young girls seemed to have been doing naturally: dressing up and imagining themselves as princesses. Seeing Disney's success at selling "25,000 Disney Princess items," other retailers (such as Mattel, owner of the Barbie franchise) have launched their own successful lines of princess merchandise.

2. As a feminist, Orenstein objects to the "princess" treatment that her three-year-old daughter receives because such behavior is so plainly a throwback to the sexist stereotypes she and other feminists fought so hard to overcome.

3. Orenstein admits to some confusion about her daughter's fascination with princesses. It is possible, she concedes, that feminism made it safe for little girls to be princesses *and* lawyers and doctors; that children, today can play act with sex-typed toys without being defined by those toys, and those roles, for their adult lives. But Orenstein seems to struggle with this possibility. She writes: "maybe I'm still surfing a washed-out second wave of feminism in a third-wave world. Maybe princesses are in fact a sign of progress, an indication that girls can embrace their predilection for pink without compromising strength or ambition; that, at long last, they can 'have it all.'"

4. Disney hired Andy Mooney to head its money-losing consumer products division. Attending a "Disney on Ice" show and, noticing an audience of little girls wearing homemade princess costumes, Mooney had the brainstorm of gathering all of the classic Disney princesses into one product line. Within six years, sales of princess merchandise reached $3 billion.

5. Responding to the accusation that princess merchandising limits girls by casting them in stereotyped roles, Mooney argues that girls and boys play in sex-typed ways and the "pass through"; that is, they explore the role and then move on to become doctors, lawyers, and professionals. These days, he says, this gender-specific role playing does not determine future behavior. Orenstein concurs: "Mooney has a point."

VIDEO LINKS

Disney's Cinderella: "A Dream is a Wish Your Heart Makes" (Sing Along)
http://www.youtube.com/watch?v=tjIssqHQJ6o

"Cinderella's Hope": Mandy More
http://www.youtube.com/watch?v=SEMdIl3d-KU&NR=1

"Cinderella": Steven Curtis Chapman
http://www.youtube.com/watch?v=tN7_qbOpuWs&feature=related

Reggae Cinderella: Errol Dunkley
http://www.youtube.com/watch?v=b0ARaI_fUjY

Cinderella Opera: Rossini
Commentary:
http://www.youtube.com/watch?v=I4O9cvoNepo
At the Ball:
http://www.youtube.com/watch?v=qQksXWFywkg&feature=related

Cinderella Ballet: Prokofiev
http://www.youtube.com/watch?v=eJisNyWDC0I

Cinderella on Broadway: Rodgers and Hammerstein "Impossible"
http://www.youtube.com/watch?v=MSDuY6BN1gM

Contemporary Movie Adaptations
Trailer for "Another Cinderella Story"
http://www.youtube.com/watch?v=vWhelh-gSA4&feature=PlayList&p=04F546497004E1BD&playnext=1&index=3

Trailer for "Ever After"
http://www.youtube.com/watch?v=Hcj9fyx6DXI

88

Chapter 13

Obedience to Authority

As with all previous editions of *Writing and Reading Across the Curriculum,* the current edition includes a chapter on obedience to authority, the central feature of which is the Milgram experiment. Four new selections—"The Power of Situations" by Lee Ross and Richard E. Nisbett, "Replicating Milgram: Would People Still Obey Today?" by Jerry M. Burger, "Group Minds" by Doris Lessing, and a scene from Ian McEwan's novel *Atonement*—have been added to this edition. The chapter addresses both the dynamics of obedience to individual authority and obedience to collective, or group authority.

When individuals refuse to relinquish any of their own autonomy for the welfare of the larger group, anarchy may result. When the state refuses individuals the right to exercise personal freedoms, totalitarianism follows. The balance that civilized people try to strike between these extremes is the territory addressed in the selections in this chapter. The chapter opens with psychoanalyst and philosopher Erich Fromm discussing the relationship between obedience and disobedience, pointing out that while acts of disobedience have spurred human development, acts of obedience can be comforting and life-affirming. This essay is especially good at alerting readers to the seductive comforts of obedience. Next, Lee Ross and Richard E. Nisbett introduce the concept of situational behavior, behavior based not on one's character but on the social cues that surround a person. Following is Milgram's account of his famous experiment with obedience: an experiment that provides one of the focal points of the chapter. Milgram conducted experiments to determine the conditions under which people can be expected to obey immoral orders—orders that appear to result in injuring people—for no justifiable reason. These experiments raised a furor and, indeed, helped lead to the development of stricter ethical guidelines for research in psychology.

Following Milgram is Jerry M. Burger's replication of Milgram's experiment with some alterations to the procedure to insure that ethical guidelines were followed. Students might want to take note that obedience to the wishes of malevolent authority appears no less problematic today, at least in laboratory settings, than when Milgram conducted his experiments in the 1960s. Then Ian

Parker's "Obedience" provides an update and an overview of the cultural impact of Milgram's experiment, the questions it raised, how it was viewed, and how the experiment's notoriety affected Milgram personally. Doris Lessing's speech, "Group Minds," alludes to some of the experiments (without specifically naming them) done on obedience in suggesting that we all succumb to group pressure, even if such pressure is unspoken. Solomon E. Asch describes a number of experiments he performed in the early 1950s which provided some foundation for the work of Stanley Milgram in the 1960s. In "The Stanford Prison Experiment," Philip G. Zimbardo describes his experiment, almost as notorious as Milgram's, in which college students randomly assigned to the roles of prisoners and prison guards quickly took on attributes associated with those roles. Like Milgram, Zimbardo feels that his findings have a number of potentially frightening implications for individuals in our society—implications students might want to explore. And the chapter closes with an episode from novelist Ian McEwan's *Atonement*—which memorably dramatizes the possible effects of what Lessing would call a "group mind" on individual behavior.

In teaching this chapter, you might emphasize one or more of the following: the social psychology experiments, obedience as it touches students' lives, or how group pressure pushes the individual to behave in ways different from how the individual would behave alone.

As with earlier chapters, this chapter contains video links relevant to the topic of obedience and its perils, including a dramatization of the famous short story "The Lottery" by Shirley Jackson. The list of links can be found at the end of this chapter.

Disobedience as a Psychological and Moral Problem (p. 683)

ERICH FROMM

Erich Fromm brings a philosophical and psychological perspective to bear on the question of obedience. Of special importance are paragraphs 13–16, in which Fromm discusses the comforts of obedience and the necessary *dis*comfort one must endure in order to disobey. Through acts of disobedience, Fromm suggests, one can become free. This concept may be difficult for students and may be worth class discussion. Working from the information in Chapter 6: Analysis, students can practice identifying the principles and definitions that Fromm establishes. You might also devote time to clarifying the distinctions Fromm

90

makes between types of obedience, types of conscience, and types of authority. His ultimate point is that any act ending in the submission of one person's will to another's or to a group's is cowardly and destructive, and any act affirming individual will and autonomy (even if this is an act of obedience, though to reason) is an act of freedom.

REVIEW QUESTIONS

1. Civilization begins, according to both the Greek and Hebrew traditions, with an act of disobedience: Adam and Eve eat the forbidden fruit; Prometheus steals the gods' sacred fire and gives it to humans. These first acts of disobedience liberated humans by forcing them to rely on and discover their own human powers. Not to have disobeyed would have meant that humans would be in nature as animals were. With no consciousness of their separateness from nature, humans would lose what makes them human.

2. Fromm refers to the disobedience of Adam and Eve (and Prometheus) as the beginning of human history (see above); the end of history may come when some military subordinate obeys orders and pushes a button that will launch a nuclear missile and precipitate a nuclear war.

3. Heteronomous obedience is the subordination of one person's will and authority to another's (or to the state's) and involves an act of submission; autonomous disobedience is the following of one's own judgment and does *not* involve submission but, rather, is an affirmation of one's moral and logical authority.

4. Authoritarian conscience is the inner voice of paternal or state authority which, through fear and intimidation, demands compliance; humanistic conscience is based on an intuitive sense of what is humane and life sustaining (as opposed to that which is inhumane and destructive). Obedience to authoritarian conscience involves submission, because the outer authority has been internalized; obedience to humanistic conscience is, by contrast, an affirmation.

5. Obedience to another person is *not* submission—that is, a negation of personal authority—if the other person is acting in the name of reason and without coercion.

6. See paragraph 13. Fromm's answer to this question is lengthy but can be summarized as follows: Obedience is, psychologically, a pleasant state since the obedient one feels protected by and can identify with the larger power or group. Authorities require obedience for economic reasons: there exist only enough treasures for the few; the desires of the many must therefore be checked, and the mechanism for such checking is obedience—not obedience based on fear (an obedience that can turn at any moment) but on desire. People obey because they wish to gain the psychological comfort of being part of a protected, and sanctioned, group.

The Power of Situations (p. 688)

LEE ROSS AND RICHARD E. NISBETT

Contrary to the idea that one's inherent character and personality traits are the deciding factors in a person's behavior, Lee Ross and Richard E. Nisbett argue that the social situations surrounding a person are far more decisive in forming the person's behavior.

REVIEW QUESTIONS

1. The "hard-won ignorance" to which the authors refer alludes to the conclusions of social psychology that contradict common sense; an example would be the "good Samaritan" experiment, the description of which begins in paragraph 3. If perceived lateness to an appointment influences whether one stops to help a person in need, then we must question our assumptions about what constitutes "helpful." This insight counts as "hard-won ignorance."

2. The main predictor of John's unwillingness to help the person slumped in the doorway was his belief in whether or not he was late for an appointment. Common sense would look to some internal state, to John's character, as a predictor of behavior. In this case, common sense would be wrong.

3. The "fundamental attribution error" is the attribution of personality traits to people (e.g., a person is "helpful," "honest," "hardworking") to explain behavior. The error in attributing dispositions does not acknowledge the ways in which a *situation* may be far more likely, in an experimentally demonstrable way, to predict behavior.

The Perils of Obedience (p. 692)

STANLEY MILGRAM

Milgram's popularized account of his experiments appeared in *Harper's* in 1973. In this piece, Milgram summarizes his experimental findings in what some might term perversely dispassionate detail. Subjects are seen anguishing over the course of action they should take; their moral dilemmas can be quite painful for readers, some of whom will—like Diana Baumrind—question the ethics of an experiment that causes such emotional distress. On finishing the selection, students should be clear on Milgram's principal experimental design and its significant variations.

Links to online versions of this article are available on the textbook's Web site, as is a summary of Milgram's experiment and Thomas Blass' "The Man Who Shocked the World," originally published in *Psychology Today*.

REVIEW QUESTIONS

1. Obedience is a basic structure of social life. Systems of authority are required by all communal living. Where authority is established, commands must be respected or anarchy will ensue. Social order is premised on a given amount of obedience.

2. The dilemma inherent in the issue of obedience is an ethical one: Why should a person obey a command that conflicts with personal conscience?

3. A summary of the obedience experiments will be based on paragraphs 4–24. Writing a summary will be tricky in that students often have difficulty articulating the difference between the experimenter's confederate—the "learner"—and the actual subject—the "teacher." We suggest that each student write a summary and then work in a group to agree on essential information. Various groups can then share their collective summaries, which, if accurate, will cover the same territory.

4. Experts predicted that virtually all subjects would refuse to continue shocking victims beyond 150 volts. Only 4% would continue to 300 volts, and only 0.1% would continue to the end of the shock board. As Milgram states: "These predictions were unequivocally wrong. Both college students at Yale and adults from the general population in New Haven were fully obedient roughly 60% of the time."

93

5. Milgram refutes these assumptions, based on an experimental design in which subjects could choose their own levels of shock (as opposed to being ordered to increase shocks incrementally). In this design, subjects overwhelmingly selected lower levels of shock, disproving (according to Milgram) the theory about innate aggressiveness. The second assumption, that only a lunatic fringe would shock learners with the maximum voltage, is undermined by Milgram's finding that nearly two-thirds of all subjects administered the maximum shock. See paragraphs 82–86.

6. Arendt contended that the portrayal of Eichmann as a sadistic monster was incorrect—that he was, rather, an uninspired, middle-level bureaucrat simply doing his job. Milgram's conclusions, that nearly two-thirds of his subjects became agents in a destructive process, seem to corroborate Arendt's thesis.

7. See paragraph 108: The essence of obedience is "that a person comes to view himself as the instrument of carrying out another person's wishes, and he therefore no longer regards himself as responsible for his actions." All essential features of obedience follow once this shift has occurred: The "agent" feels responsibility to the figure of authority, not to the victim.

8. When subjects did not need to take direct responsibility for inflicting painful shocks, 36 of 40 proceeded in their roles—resulting in the learners being shocked at the maximum level.

9. It was a fragmentation of the total human act that led to the atrocities of the concentration camps in World War II. Eichmann shuffled papers and gave orders that he did not have to see carried out; thus he did not face the direct effects of his actions. Persons at the other end of the chain of command, those who actually gassed victims, could claim that they were merely following orders, thus relieving themselves of the responsibility for their acts. With no one person responsible for the total act (i.e., designing and implementing the Final Solution), no one person was forced to live with the ramifications of that act. Every person in the chain had a convenient means of absolving himself or herself of guilt.

Replicating Milgram: Would People Still Obey Today? (p. 702)

JERRY M. BURGER

This selection is excerpted from Jerry M. Burger's article, which provides a crisp review of the ethical concerns raised by Milgram's experiment, a replication of that experiment (within established ethical guidelines), and the conclusions Burger reached, similar to those reached by Milgram.

REVIEW QUESTIONS

1. Burger "predicted that any differences in obedience between the 1961-1962 participants (Milgram, 1963) and the 2006 participants would be minimal." His hypothesis was confirmed.

2. The "150-volt solution" was the primary mechanism by which Burger avoided the ethical concerns raised by the original obedience experiments. In Milgram's studies, subjects were willing to apply what they thought were shocks through to the last switch on the shock generator, marked 450 volts. Milgram's results showed that 79% of those who went past the 150-volt level continued "to the end of the shock generator's range." Burger made a "reasonable estimate" that he could end his experiment after participants reached the 150-volt level, figuring they would at that point likely continue on to 450 volts. Burger put the 150-volt solution into place to spare subjects the psychological trauma that may have been experienced by Milgram's subjects.

3. Burger's "base condition" attempted to recreate with a high degree of fidelity Milgram's own experimental conditions—to the extent that the experimenter in the study and the confederate resembled the experimenter and the confederate in the original study. As well, Burger used for the experiment "a script taken largely from the one used in Milgram's research." In the "modeled refusal condition," the base condition was modified to add a second confederate—a "teacher" who would administer shocks alongside the true subject. At 90 volts, this teacher refused to continue the experiment, as the true subject watched. The experimenter then instructed the subject to continue administering shocks.

4. Burger summarized his results in Tables 2 and 3. In the base condition, 70% of participants were willing to proceed after 150 volts, and the experiment

95

had to be terminated. In the modeled refusal condition, 63% were willing to continue. These results did not differ significantly from Milgram's findings. The experiments showed no significant difference between the responses of male and female subjects.

5. Burger set out to re-test Milgram's findings on the power of situations to influence behavior. Social psychologists have shown experimentally—see Asch, Zimbardo, and the "Good Samaritan" experiment reported by Ross and Nisbett—that pressures embedded in situations involving other people can greatly influence a person's behavior—more so, even than the person's supposed character traits. Notwithstanding the example of a co-teacher who refused to continue with shocking the learner, 63% of Burger's subjects continued with the experiment. The situational forces at work—the insistent demands of the experimenter that the participant must continue—proved a stronger influence on the subject's behavior than did the modeled refusal.

Obedience (p. 709)

IAN PARKER

Parker's article provides background on Milgram's attempts to publish his study and can be valuable as an opening to a discussion of scholarly work. Students would be helped by a discussion of the role of academic journals in furthering scholarly research. They would also benefit from a discussion on the difference between a peer-reviewed journal and a popular magazine in terms of the level of authority, the rationale for publication, and the care taken in reviewing research. They should also notice that Milgram revised his initial work in response to editorial suggestions and that some of his conclusions became lost as the research gained popular attention. Additionally, it took ten years before he was able to fully conceptualize his ideas in his book. A discussion of these topics will help students understand the importance of tracing research back to the original publication whenever possible, and of making the effort to use journals as sources, rather than depending on newspaper and Internet accounts.

The discussion of the impact of Holocaust studies on Milgram's work shows how contextual influences (e.g., Eichmann's trial, Arendt's book, and My Lai) shape the direction of an idea's reception as it works its way through newspaper accounts and television, becomes the focus of debates on human subjects' experimental guidelines and, finally, having taken a life of its own, impacts Milgram's career.

96

Having considered the impact of Milgram's experiment on American culture, Parker then examines Orne, Holland and Goldhagen's methodological questions, reflecting the normal academic research process, the way scholarly research is supposed to be treated. This is followed by Ross and Nisbett's reinterpretation of the meaning of the "Milgram situation." This reinterpretation of the experiment's lessons is, in turn, reflected by Parker back to how the response to the experiment affected Milgram's professional career.

REVIEW QUESTIONS

1. Editors rejected Milgram's first version of his paper because it described only one experimental situation, without any variables or variant situations. Without such variant versions of the procedure, Milgram's findings were considered a "demonstration," rather than an "experiment."

2. The basic defense of the Nazi officials charged at Nuremberg was that they were just following orders. This was also the essential explanation given by many of Milgram's subjects for continuing to administer shocks to the learner even when they thought that the learner might be suffering considerable harm. Milgram postulated that the people following orders did so not because they were inherently evil; on the contrary, they were, for the most part, quite ordinary. Rather, they continued to obey the insistent experimenter because they believed that ordinary people should follow orders.

3. The obedience experiments ruined Milgram's career since he was never able to live them down. With many social science professionals questioning the morality, the procedures, and the validity of the experiments, Milgram's career was stunted: he failed to get tenure at Harvard and taught for the rest of his career at an institution (the Graduate Center of the City University of New York) that was generally considered a step down from the Ivy League institutions where he began his career.

4. In his title, *Hitler's Willing Executioners*, Daniel Goldhagen implies a state of mind different from that of Milgram's subjects and our image of Nazis and ordinary German citizens just following orders. In Goldhagen's view, Germans and Poles killed Jews less because they had been ordered to do so by superiors and were reluctantly following orders, but rather because they truly believed that Jews were inferior, even evil, and thus deserved death.

5. In making his charge that Milgram's experiment is "not scientific, it's . . . *scientistic*," Stam suggests that Milgram's results were achieved only because of the carefully controlled conditions of a laboratory experiment. In the real world, there are too many other variables (such as trust, and the way that most people actually make decisions) for Milgram's experimental results to indicate or account for the way that people actually behave.

Group Minds (p. 720)

DORIS LESSING

This selection is excerpted from a speech Doris Lessing delivered in 1985, one of five lectures she gave as part of the William E. Massey, Sr., Lectures on the History of American Civilization at Harvard University. It concerns the disparity between how we think of ourselves as independent individuals with independent thoughts and independent behavior and how we really are as members of social groups who act according to the pressures of the group. We can see this illustrated not only in several experiments detailed in this chapter but also in the excerpt from McEwan's novel *Atonement* (742). This speech, together with the other four delivered in the lecture series, was later incorporated into the collection *Prisons We Choose to Live Inside* (1987). Lessing was awarded the Nobel Prize in Literature in 2007.

REVIEW QUESTIONS

1. Lessing writes that people living in the West think of themselves as free agents: as individuals free of any gross influences on their behaviors by others. That is, people in the West believe they enjoy unfettered free will. Lessing points out that this is not the case and that our behavior is shaped by unexamined social forces of the kind discussed by Milgram, Asch, and Zimbardo in this chapter.

2. Lessing believes that individuals in the West are "helpless against all kinds of pressures on them to conform in many kinds of ways." Why?

3. Lessing refers to a class of experiments on obedience. Summarize the "typical" experiment: A subject is unwittingly influenced by confederates of the experimenter—that is, in an experimental setting, social pressures are brought to bear on the subject—to make judgments contrary to his moral sense or his perceptual sense. The experiment is designed to determine how likely, and under what conditions, the subject will contradict what he

98

believes to be true or right in order to conform to a group's, or a power figure's, wishes. In the case of the Asch experiment, group pressure leads a subject to say line A is shorter than line B when the subject is certain that the opposite is true. Yet in an effort to conform to the group decision, the subject will in effect lie so as not to appear to be contrary or disruptive.

Opinions and Social Pressure (p. 723)

SOLOMON E. ASCH

In this selection, Asch describes an apparently simple experiment in which college students are asked to make statements about what they saw, not knowing that the actual test observed how well they resisted a group consensus which challenged their judgments. Asch examines the variables which could affect an individual's ability to resist group pressure and raises concerns about the dangers of too much conformity in our society. He also ends on a fairly optimistic note as to the ability of the individual to resist conformity. Students should consider whether they agree with Asch's optimism at this point, and then reconsider their views in light of the findings of Milgram and Zimbardo.

REVIEW QUESTIONS

1. "Suggestibility" is a psychological process by which people may undergo physiological changes or may be induced to perform certain actions as a result of the reiteration of instructions. Thus, it is a form of hypnotic state, except that the person may be fully awake. Social pressure can, without any explicit reiteration of instructions, become the agent that induces such a state in an individual.

2. Responses will vary but all should cover the essential procedures and results of the experiment. The summaries should describe both the stated and the real purpose of the experiment (stated: an experiment about visual acuity; real: an experiment about social pressure); they should include the number of people involved in the experiment (seven to nine, in each of 18 trails, for a total of 123); and they should describe the essential procedure requiring the subjects to select the one line out of three on a card that matched in length the single line on another card. The summaries may note that, in order to avoid raising the suspicions of the subject, the experimenter's confederates initially—and occasionally later in the experiment—did give correct answers. The results showed that under group pressure, subjects were induced to give incorrect answers 36.8% of the time. From these results, Asch concluded that

individuals are remarkably, perhaps even dangerously, susceptible to group pressure, giving answers they know to be wrong, rather than buck the majority.

3. Asch found that reducing the size of the majority drastically reduced the degree of susceptibility of the subjects. With the support of even one partner, the subject reduced his incorrect answers by 75%.

4. While both consensus and conformity involve agreement among individuals in a group, the two are quite different. In a condition of consensus, each individual has arrived at a conclusion based upon his or her own best judgment, a judgment that happens to coincide with that of other members of the group. In a condition of conformity, on the other hand, individuals reach a state of agreement primarily because potential dissenters don't want to stand apart from the group, don't want to appear different or troublesome. Consensus is productive, according to Asch; conformity involves a degree of mindlessness that is potentially dangerous.

The Stanford Prison Experiment (p. 729)

PHILIP G. ZIMBARDO

This selection describes another important experiment in social psychology. The focus of the experiment was on obedience to roles, in this case the roles of prisoner and prison guard. The article is written in a discursive style, and students might want to begin by summarizing the elements of the experiment. As this experiment has many similarities to, as well as differences from, Milgram's study, students can also compare and contrast the two: the experimental design, the issues investigated, the ethical issues raised, and the findings and conclusions. If students read the critiques of Milgram's experiments, they might attempt to critique the Stanford prison experiment along these or other lines. In his final paragraphs, Zimbardo discusses implications for daily life. To what extent do students agree with these implications? Do they see other implications for daily life? In view of the explosive growth of the prison population, students might also look at the implications of the experiment for the immediate subject: prison life.

A link to the Stanford Prison Experiment Web site and other related links are provided on the textbook's Web site. Additionally, there are links to an interview with Philip Zimbardo by Christina Maslach and a collection of links devoted to the BBC's broadcast, "The Experiment," a documentary that attempts to replicate elements of Zimbardo's study.

REVIEW QUESTIONS

1. Zimbardo "sought to understand more about the process by which people called 'prisoners' lose their liberty, civil rights, independence and privacy, while those called 'guards' gain social power by accepting the responsibility for controlling and managing the lives of their dependent charges" (paragraph 7).

2. Zimbardo's subjects were judged "to be emotionally stable, physically healthy, mature, law-abiding citizens" (paragraph 9). They were "average, middle-class, Caucasian, college-age males" (paragraph 10). Zimbardo emphasizes the point that his subjects were representative of college-age males nationwide. This representation allows him to generalize his findings at the end of the article.

3. The psychological process of becoming a prisoner is a response, says Zimbardo, to a systematic attempt to strip individuals of all positive associations with self. Having conducted extensive interviews and reviewed journal literature on prison, Zimbardo (paragraph 13) writes that a prisoner feels "powerless, arbitrarily controlled, dependent, frustrated, hopeless, anonymous, dehumanized and emasculated." Zimbardo designed a physical space and set of interactions between guards and prisoners that would achieve these psychological ends. Over time, the social setting, with its strictly separated roles and behaviors, "de-individualized" (paragraph 17) both prisoners and guards. There developed a "perverted symbiotic relationship" (paragraph 19), as prisoners willingly succumbed to the arbitrary control of prison guards and guards willingly took on feelings associated with authority.

4. In paragraph 19, Zimbardo reports on the "perverted symbiotic relationship" that developed between prisoners and guards, who came to display complementary psychological traits. Guards became active, prisoners passive and dependent; guards became self-important, prisoners self-effacing; guards became powerful and controlling, prisoners hopeless.

5. The prisoners "rioted" during the second day of the experiment: they barricaded themselves in the cells and ripped off their prisoner numbers. The

guards responded with force, discharging a fire extinguisher at them. The guards stripped the prisoners, separated them into "good" and "bad" groups, and then switched group members arbitrarily so that prisoners could no longer trust one another not to inform. The guards developed insidiously effective means of control; the prisoners caved in psychologically and did not pose a further security risk. See paragraphs 23–28.

6. Prisoners could not have respect for other prisoners, says Zimbardo, because the system they inhabited did not permit them to get to know one another as individuals. Each prisoner saw others behaving "like compliant sheep [and] carrying out mindless orders" (paragraph 31). Given the circumstances, prisoners could not respect either their fellows or themselves.

7. Guard A's journal reveals an astonishing transformation from one who initially describes himself as "a political pacifist and nonaggressive individual" into a brutal individual who could "single [a prisoner] out for special abuse" because he thinks the prisoner "begs for it" and he (Guard A) doesn't like him. A social system transformed representative college students into brutal mock-guards and obsequious mock-prisoners. The transformation was so compelling and complete that Zimbardo called an early end to the experiment, which lasted six of the planned 14 days.

8. At the end of his article, Zimbardo suggests that people may willingly take on the role of prisoner because it gives them an excuse to be passive and take direction. Those who accept the orders of others do not see themselves as responsible for their own actions.

9. Zimbardo suggests that individuals acting in tightly structured social systems readily adopt the role assigned to them. Once taken on, the role becomes something of a prison, a mental box out of which the individual will not venture. Zimbardo extends his research to suggest that one can be a mental prisoner of marriage, a prisoner of shyness, and so on. The environment creates the external structure for the prison; the individual creates an internal psychology for being a prisoner (or a guard)—and the system perpetuates itself, with attendant degradations and harm.

From Atonement *(p. 742)*

IAN MCEWAN

Ian McEwan captures the dilemma of an individual, Turner, caught up in a crowd's frenzy. As the crowd of soldiers converges on a lone RAF pilot to blame him for not having protected their dead compatriots from German bombers, Turner finds himself frozen, caught between wanting to help the pilot and being tempted to join in the physical attacks against him.

There are no review questions for this selection.

VIDEO LINKS

Asch and Milgram
        Asch Conformity Experiment
        http://www.youtube.com/watch?v=R6LH10-3H8k

        Milgram Re-enactment: from "The Heist"
        http://www.youtube.com/watch?v=y6GxIuljT3w

        Candid Camera "Under Pressure"
        http://www.youtube.com/watch?v=WPfMpatUQIA&feature=related

Zimbardo
        Stanford Prison Experiment
        http://www.youtube.com/watch?v=JxGEmfNl-xM

        Interview w/ Zimbardo
        http://www.youtube.com/watch?v=F-ULKNziT2w&feature=related

        Zimbardo on the "Lucifer Effect"
        http://www.youtube.com/watch?v=OsFEV35tWsg&feature=related

Shirley Jackson, "The Lottery"
        Part I
        http://www.youtube.com/watch?v=tN5V8cQ2DAk

        Part II
        http://www.youtube.com/watch?v=UMOMcO0vlfo&feature=related